The Touch Crisis

Navigating the Tricky Terrain of Bringing Healthy Touch Back to Our Culture

by
Dawn Bennett

TOUCH REMEDIES

The Touch Crisis
Navigating the Tricky Terrain of Bringing Healthy Touch Back to Our Culture

Published by
Touch Remedies
Stillwater, MN

www.TouchRemedies.com

Copyright © 2020 by Dawn Bennett

Cover by Dan Mulhern
Interior Design by Dawn Teagarden

All rights reserved. No part of this book may be reproduced or transmitted in any form or by any means, electronic or mechanical, including photocopying, recording, or by an information storage and retrieval system without written permission of the publisher, except for the inclusions of brief quotations in review.

Disclaimer: The Publisher and the Author does not guarantee that anyone following the techniques, suggestions, tips, ideas or strategies will become successful. The advice and strategies contained herein may not be suitable for every situation. The Publisher and Author shall have neither liability nor responsibility to anyone with respect to any loss or damage caused, or alleged to be caused, directly or indirectly by the information in this book. Permission has been obtained to share the identity of each real individual named in this book.

Any citations or a potential source of information from other organizations or websites given herein does not mean that the Author or Publisher endorses the information/content the website or organization provides or recommendations it may make. It is the readers' responsibility to do their own due diligence when researching information. Also, websites listed or referenced herein may have changed or disappeared from the time that this work was created and the time that it is read.

ISBN: 9798674501411

Printed in the United States of America
www.TouchRemedies.com

WHAT READERS ARE SAYING

"During my first read through *The Touch Crisis*, I felt a resistance to the exercises the author introduced and chose to ignore them. By the time I had finished the book, Dawn's story had opened my heart and revealed my overwhelming fear of rejection... a fear that had been masking and numbing my need for touch. The second time through, the exercises empowered and enabled me to rewrite my 'rejection' story. Now I use this book as a resource and pick it up periodically to hunt for the part that I need to re-read, a part that ministers to where I am now, today. Thank you, Dawn, for sharing your journey and helping me begin healing my own touch crisis."

Theddee Rheyshelle
Author and Spiritual Coach

"Touch is one of my top love languages, so this topic is close to my heart. This book is filled with personal, relatable real-life stories as well as a lot of research. Dawn's a gifted writer, and she kept me wanting to turn the page. I also very much appreciate the exercises in the book, so we can apply these teachings to our daily life."

Elda Dorothy
CompassionateTruth.com

"*The Touch Crisis* offers a transformative experience, no matter where your relationship with touch is at this moment. Dawn's story drew me into a world of intention, exploration, growth, and healing. To heal is a journey and this book makes a perfect travel companion."

Leah Buysse
Owner, Indigo Health & Wellness

"This book will take you on a grand adventure and down paths you've never traveled. Through Dawn's exquisite grasp of connection (or lack thereof), you'll explore your fears, joys, or resistance to touch. Whether you're a 'hugger' or prefer to abstain, this book will enhance every encounter you have."

Laura McDonough
Victim Assistance/
Restorative Justice Program,
MN DOC (ret)

"In this book, Dawn puts her personal experience of touch under a microscope. We see her struggles laid bare. We see her emotions get intense. And we see her return safely to herself. For me, this glimpse of 'what healthy looks like on the inside' is what I especially liked about *The Touch Crisis*."

Frank Barr
Retired Psychologist

*To all who have overcome their touch
challenges and to those who strive to do so.*

ACKNOWLEDGMENTS

To those who have helped me look inside myself and heal, this book would never have made it to paper without you.

To My Family

To my parents. You watched with love as I created my own challenges and made tons of mistakes. You tried hard to understand what I was studying, doing, practicing, and healing in myself every step of my journey. You gave me hugs, taught me how to fix houses and cars, and you modeled how to be real with people. You supported me even as I "dropped out of college," dated questionable people, quit my business, got married, got divorced, created new businesses, and moved to Europe… twice. You've laughed at my jokes since I was a child and still do (the cow has the udder one!). You supported me every single step of the way, even though you have shared around the campfire that you really had no clue what on earth I was doing or where I would end up. And now here we are, with parts of our lives laid out in a book for everyone to see. Some of this will be new to you, as I keep my struggles and emotions pretty tight to my chest—until we get around the campfire. I am a strong, independent, and passionate woman because of the two of you as individuals and as a couple. I couldn't have asked for better parents and a better support system. Thank you from the bottom of my heart. I love you both very deeply.

To my sister. I wasn't the best older sister I could have been when we were younger, or even through much of our college years. Thanks for putting up with my shenanigans and my bossiness, and for doing lots of my chores when I was babysitting you. I am so grateful we have built a stronger relationship as adults, and am grateful for our communication and your forgiveness. I only hope that I can be the role model and support for your children that I could have been with you... and more.

To my brother. We didn't grow up together, but I hope this answers some of your deeper questions about how I think about life and how I came to be who I am today. I look forward to building a stronger relationship with you and your family as the years pass.

To those friends who I consider family—Chris, Ross, Jake, Lisa, Gabriella, Carli, Trish, and Frank (and so many others who have popped in and out of my life to teach me something, no matter how briefly). Some of you have known me over twenty years, and others have known me a relatively short while; but all of you supported me and saw me through something big. Your support, thought-provoking conversations, and way-of-being inspire me to do more, to challenge myself, to stay strong to my spirit. You help me find safety and security when I am in the depth of confusion, personal change, and even self-sabotage. In your own ways, you remind me to look at others with light and love, and to take care of my needs before others (even when I choose not to listen). You've provided home, shoulders to cry on, and places to dance, laugh, ponder life, and transform. You have all taught me something deeper about myself, and it brings tears to my eyes just knowing you are all out there bringing better things to this world—some of it through this book.

To Those Represented in This Book

Most of you know who you are. Thank you for the ways you have touched my life. Thank you for listening as I shared the role you play in this book. Even though I expose our challenges, I am a better person today because of each of you and am grateful for the experiences we share together.

I appreciate all of you who shared your stories, tips, tricks, and lessons during our interviews. To Thomas and Sara, to Marcia B and Betty M, for bringing me even farther along my journey of finding the best practices in touch.

To My Team Who Keeps Me Safe and on My Path

To the many people who gave me a safe place, even if only for a few days, to call home while I was writing this book and stepping into a higher level of myself: Gabriela, Håkan, Liz, Carina, The Powells, Carli, Rob, Marcia, Jan and Terry, Sue, Madeleine and Pierre-Jean, and Jake. I wouldn't have had such clarity, nor such opportunity, if it were not for all of you.

To Jason-Aeric, my homeopath and mentor, the one who has been instrumental in hearing the depth of my pain, reflecting the spaces I have been stuck, and helping to uncover my true spirit. Many people have walked with me on my healing journey, but you have been the most consistent and the one who reflects depth in a way no one else has. Thank you for reminding me to "Be Loved."

To Amanda Johnson, my amazing writing coach, guide, and witness, who kept me on track, who let me know that "maybe the reason chapter five is not coming is that you are catching up with your timeline and have something else to learn." Who observed my pain as it came forward and supported me lovingly from the other side of the world while I struggled for a way to be vulnerable enough to share it in a way that could help others. Who was patient with me when I was not patient with her.

Thank you, Ursula, for recommending Amanda, and for the years of coaching that led up to this book.

To My Clients and My Community

I am not exaggerating when I say I love you all. I have done the best I can to support, nurture, and hold space for you. Thank you for being patient as I transformed myself multiple times, changed my offerings, moved away, shifted hours, ran late, and made mistakes. Thanks for the reminders when you saw I was working too much and trying to get three bites of food in during my five-minute breaks that I need to take care of myself, too.

Thanks to Kik and Steve for being my business equivalent to home.

Thank you to the women who after my presentations said, "You should write a book about this." So many of you shared how my simple suggestions back then have changed your world. Thank you for sharing your own struggles and desires as you brought healthier touch into your own lives.

With All My Love and Gratitude,

Dawn Bennett

CONTENTS

15
Introduction | Planning Your Journey
Breaking News: COVID-19

45
Chapter 1 | Ruts & Remedies

73
Chapter 2 | Routes & Resources

109
Chapter 3 | Crossroads & Choices

145
Chapter 4 | Yodels & Poles

209
Chapter 5 | Campfires & Cookouts

275
Conclusion | Our Path Forward
The Statistics In the Time of COVID

287
About Dawn Bennett

291
A Special Invitation from Dawn

293
Extra Resources

297
Climb Higher | The Play & Explore Workbook

323
Endnotes

"We need 4 hugs a day for survival. We need 8 hugs a day for maintenance. We need 12 hugs a day for growth."

~ Virginia Satir, American author and family therapist ~

INTRODUCTION
PLANNING YOUR JOURNEY

I had just dropped my rucksack on the bedroom floor and stepped into the bright, open hallway when I heard the ruckus. I peeked over the open stairwell and saw my two nephews pounding up the stairs with excitement, the six-year-old, Geoffrey, a few paces ahead of his younger brother.

"Auntie Dawn! Auntie Dawn!" I knelt down to receive the oncoming barrage of love, and my heart nearly burst with happiness when I saw his sweet face round the corner. His brown hair bounced as he ran toward me, his green eyes sparkling with glee, a giant smile on his face.

He almost knocked me over as he ran into me full-force for a giant hug. I wrapped my arms around his little frame as soon as he crashed into me. His brother joined from the left side, blonde curls framing his sticky face, and snuck in for a group hug. As I gave them both a big squeeze, overwhelmed by the outpouring of love from their big hearts, I wanted to hold onto them forever.

"Auntie Dawn, I missed you! Are you going away again?" Geoffrey's tiny voice was strained with anxiety.

Oh no, I thought, surprised by the length and ferocity of his hug as I held him close. I was suddenly feeling polarized between the immense amount of love flowing between us and the intruding guilt sinking into my stomach. *I didn't think it mattered to him that I was gone for nine months. They don't see me that often anyway.*

Suddenly, the two large dogs descended on the three of us, tails wagging and tongues flying, trying to get in on the action. As the youngest let go and started asking questions, Geoffrey kept me locked in his arms with an intensity I hadn't felt from him before.

I don't want to be another person in his life who comes and goes and makes him feel unstable, unloved, or disconnected. I thought we stayed really connected over FaceTime. I guess that wasn't enough.

As I held him close, trying to reconcile the overwhelming energy of the dogs, the barrage of questions from the youngest, and the increasing concern about him, images and sounds of a different memory emerged—reminding me of the last time a wonderful hug led to questions about connection and my responsibilities within it.

Dropped Into the Wild

"Hi there! Nice to see you!" I exclaimed cheerfully, as I walked toward a fellow businesswoman on my way back to my wellness center. It was a sunny winter day in Minnesota and we were both in our warm jackets and hats, the fog from our breath drifting lazily upward.

"Dawn, I would like to talk with you." Her normally bright voice sounded a bit serious, and I paused to give her the proper space to voice whatever was on her mind.

I nodded affirmatively, as I sipped coffee from the warm cup I'd just picked up from the café down the street. *I wonder what's wrong.*

"Well, I was at the award ceremony a few weeks ago," she started.

Immediately, I felt my whole body warm at the memory and a large smile overtook my face. The business I had grown from scratch had been given the "Service Business of the Year" award by the Chamber of Commerce.

"I thought you behaved unprofessionally, hugging everyone at that event." Her voice was matter-of-fact and empty of any emotion.

What? I felt my heart drop as confusion overwhelmed me and my face flushed with heat.

"The way you hugged people that night was completely inappropriate," she scolded.

My mind quickly retrieved the vivid memory of that evening in the decorated casino ballroom, recalling how elated I was—how surprised and honored that enough people had felt connected to and nurtured by my staff and me that they had voted for us. I had bounced around the full tables of professionals on my way to the stage to accept the award and thank everyone, thinking Grammy winners couldn't have been more excited.

After my gushing yet short speech, I'd floated off the stage in a cloud of pride and love, making eye contact with those I knew and hugging at least fifteen of my friends on the way back to my seat, consciously restraining myself to not hug *everyone* I knew. After I settled back in at my table, I had given hugs to my two staff members seated next to me.

She interrupted my thoughts again, "I'm just trying to help you understand that is no way to act in a business setting."

What is she talking about? Is it really offensive to hug people I know in a moment like that? Is she right? Did I offend people? Should I not be hugging people in these settings—ever? I felt my body start retreating into numbness as the impact of her words set in.

Reconstructing the Rutted Trail

My nephew tightened his arms one more time before he pulled away, looked me in the eyes, and asked, "Are you spending the night? Will you jump on the trampoline with us?"

"Of course," I replied enthusiastically, shaking my head to clear the memory as I stood up and walked with them to the stairs. "I am super excited to play with you two!"

As I played with them and interacted with the rest of my family that evening, I thought about how far I had come since that moment on the street.

I went from being enthusiastic with my hugs and affection and encouraging my clients (especially those who had experienced touch challenges and abuse) to speak their needs and find strong boundaries, to withdrawing from almost all touch myself. I didn't bounce back as quickly as I did when I was twenty-two years old and Diane told me she didn't like being touched and didn't want me to hug her or her boyfriend anymore. I'd felt bad then that my actions had made her uncomfortable, and I'd made changes around my actions on a larger scale; but twelve years later, being accused of inappropriate touch rocked me to my core.

As a human who craves a lot of physical touch—and as a professional whose business was all about therapeutic healing touch—it called a lot of my life experience into question and made me terrified to make a mistake until

I got it all sorted out. The last thing I wanted to do was harm anyone.

I spent several years unpacking the intense emotions and answering the many questions that emerged from that brief interaction on the street, which I have come to call the "shaming incident," because of how deeply it affected me and made me question myself.

As I scouted my inner terrain for all of the assumptions and experiences that had forged my relationship to touch, I discovered that even though I was vigilant about intention and safety with my clients, I had a lot of room to grow in creating and maintaining safety for myself and loved ones in my personal life.

There were a number of unexpected moments and discoveries, but the one that really changed the trajectory of my personal and professional life started with a 2016 article in the New Yorker Magazine[1] about the importance of touch, especially related to haptic technology, which creates an experience of touch for a user. For example, prosthetic hands that can "feel" texture, shape, and temperature.

The science of touch communication, and why touch is so important to humans of all ages absolutely fascinated me and confirmed my observations over twenty years in a high-touch profession.

Before I go any further, let me clarify what I am referring to when I use the word "touch." I am referring to all forms of consensual, healthy, physical communication and contact between people. From casual handshakes and high-fives in professional or community situations, to holding hands, putting a compassionate hand on someone's shoulder, and hugs in more familiar or close interpersonal interactions.

I already knew from my bodywork training how touch could stimulate memories and assist with the release of emotions stored in tissues, and how the body has a wisdom that can communicate what it needs to release/heal symptoms that seem completely unrelated to stressful past events. I had even read Peter Levine's book, *Waking the Tiger*, and his research into how the nervous system stores trauma and ways to release it gently and safely and effectively had intrigued me.

What I had observed but not researched until I was well into my own personal healing around the "shaming incident," was the science of how touch impacts our society as a whole. The New Yorker article introduced me to statistics I had never seen that showed how consensual touch helps with brain development in seven- and eight-year-olds. I had never read about the importance of touch for adults and how a study in the NBA correlated the success of a team with the number of times they touched each other preseason. I had never considered using touch technology to connect people that lived far from each other to help them feel connected and alive.

Learning about the health and cultural benefits of touch further stimulated my desire to understand how we communicate, or don't, our touch wants and needs, and how we can possibly keep safe and consensual touch in our circles. I decided I needed to learn to communicate my needs to my family and friends, as well as become clearer around asking others in my broader circles if they wanted touch or a hug in a way that made them feel safe. I had rarely ever asked for a hug. I just went in for one; and if I wanted one and if the opportunity did not present itself, I would just suffer in silence. I had to tackle my own mountain of wants, needs, and consent and get really honest with myself about how my words and behaviors would have to change so I could enjoy more healthy touch in my life. Eventually, I had to scale the challenges of communicating (rather clumsily) my new realizations to those around me and acquire a number of healing tools to help me navigate the tricky terrain of inner and outer relationships.

Excited about the possibility of helping women heal their touch stories and integrate more healthy touch in their lives, I started speaking at women's groups about touch. That's when *The Touch Crisis* in our culture became painfully clear to me and inspired me to speak up at a much larger and louder level than I had ever imagined.

I listened to teachers report the agony of not being able to touch kids when they hugged them. They had to avoid touch so they would not lose their job; they believed those kids who needed touch so desperately were looking for some kind of bonding, reassurance, and touch connection because they came from low-touch families; and they felt they were dampening the childrens' ability to be spontaneously loving and generous.

I heard about brothers and sisters who got into trouble for touching on the playground.

I listened to people's confusion about touch boundaries in the workplace and how to ask for touch, refuse touch, or clarify boundaries.

I heard about how sometimes people do not know what they want or need because their internal wants conflict with societal messaging, and how it had created fear, discomfort, and even shame.

It saddened me to hear that children and adults of all ages are going without the touch they crave. As a person who loves physical contact, I feel it is terrible to have another person dictate to you when you can and cannot have it if they are not directly involved. It angered me that this is happening primarily because we live in a society where touch has become a challenging, if not taboo, topic; and people are suffering because there is no cultural conversation or leader to help navigate it. And it absolutely frightened me when I put the science of touch next to the statistics in the United States.

Let's start with the science!

Although I'm not a scientist, I have read numerous books and research studies; viewed lectures from specialists around the world; taken classes on the science of the brain, touch, trauma, and healing using touch; and observed the power of touch, in both positive and negative senses, with community and clients. Plus, with more than twenty years in a touch and healing field, I have heard and seen the cause and effect of good touch communication and interactions that are just starting to be fully understood as researchers evaluate the science of the hormones, nature versus nurture, and the exact mechanisms of touch.

Looking at the science available today, there are many correlations between touch and individual and community health that are well-documented, including how intentional consensual touch increases development in the bodies and brains of our young. It gives children a more positive feeling around themselves and their body. It creates calmness, trust, and feelings of connection between adult friends and strangers alike. This made me question some of those "no-touch" policies that I was hearing about from my clients who work with children; and I quickly found that these policies, originally designed to protect children, may be more harmful than we've been led to believe.

The Science

- "A study we conducted on touch in preschool nurseries revealed that children under the age of five were being touched less than 12 percent of the time, even in model nursery schools"[2] and that "no touch mandates do not seem to reduce child abuse,"[3] said Tiffany Field, Director of the Touch Research Institute and Professor in the Departments of Pediatrics, Psychology, and Psychiatry at the University of Miami School of Medicine, in her book *Touch (A Bradford Book)*.

- "More frequent partner hugs and higher oxytocin levels are linked to lower blood pressure and heart rate in premenopausal women,"[4] according to a University of North Carolina study.

- In a study of how children 7 to 10 years old play together, Dr. Sandra Weiss, a professor at the University of California Medical School, found that rough-housing seemed to give children more positive feelings about themselves and a more accurate sense of their bodies.[5]

- There is "... a disproportionate incidence of physical abuse and **neglect** or **the lack of positive physical contact** in violent individuals,"[6] according to research done by Tiffany Field in 2002.

- In a randomized, double blind, placebo-controlled study it was found "... oxytocin administration reduces aggressive behavior in healthy young men."[7]

Physical contact has also been proven to be imperative in families as well. Studies have even suggested that increased levels of oxytocin (one of the many chemicals in the body released during touch) in men contributes to fidelity.

Without touch (or with challenging/abusive touch), infants and children do not develop as well, are less likely to form strong trusting social bonds, and tend to be more withdrawn. As people become older and these touch patterns continue, there is a strong correlation between increased rates of violence, a disconnect from or distrust of others, and less pro-social and pro-community types of behaviors. It's thought that this is due to the fact that touch releases oxytocin, a hormone produced in the hypothalamus of the brain.

MORE ABOUT OXYTOCIN

Various studies show other roles the hormone oxytocin, also known as the "cuddling hormone," plays in the body such as reducing stress, decreasing drug cravings, and increasing the immune system's ability to prevent disease. It is used in injections for contractions during labor and to reduce bleeding after childbirth, but it is also shown to be important for bonding children with their caregivers. It is important to developing a sense of connection and well-being. There is even research being done to study oxytocin's effects on helping people with autism and anxiety. Low oxytocin has also been linked to depression.[8]

> **DID YOU KNOW?**
> **THE STUDIES SHOW**
>
> Additional benefits of touch include:
>
> - A decrease in blood pressure
> - Increased building of neurological brain pathways
> - A decrease in the stress hormone cortisol
> - Better sleep
> - A movement in the brain and body from a fight/flight to a rest state
> - A decrease in the sense of loneliness
> - An expansion of social empathy
> - Stronger teamwork practices in play and work situations
> - ...and so much more

Even Maslow's hierarchy of needs rates the need for connection and belonging as the first level of psychological needs after our basic survival and safety are met.[9]

It's time for us to wake up!

Loneliness has been declared a public health crisis as the rates drastically increase. Studies show around half of Americans report feeling lonely some or all of the time.[10] According to the Cigna U.S. Loneliness

Index, "Loneliness has the same impact on mortality as smoking 15 cigarettes a day, making it even more dangerous than obesity."[11] Suicide ideation, parasuicide, and depression also increase with the degree of loneliness;[12] and the U.S. suicide rate increased by 30% overall (50% in women and girls) between 2000 and 2016.[13] Although neither living alone nor social media use are predictors of loneliness, teen depression and suicide have skyrocketed since 2011.

Additionally, although official statistics show a current decrease overall in violent crime since 1990,[14] there are still some shocking statistics to consider when it comes to violence in our culture. "While aggravated assault is the only assault category included under violent crime reports in the US, other nations include the much more numerous 'level 1' assault in violent crime reporting. This makes the U.S. appear relatively less violent from a statistical perspective."[15] Yet in the United States, "gun murders rose 32% between 2014 and 2017,"[16] and "after many years of nearly uninterrupted declines, the national rates for violent crime and homicide increased from 2014 to 2016."[17] "One category is in the midst of a slow but persistent six-year upward swing: rape."[18]

The Statistics

- The 2020 Cigna U.S. Loneliness and the Workplace report states: "Fifty-eight percent of respondents say they always or sometimes feel like no one knows them well, up four percentage points from 2018 (54%). More than half (52%) report sometimes or always feeling alone, up six percentage points from 2018 (46%). Those reporting that they feel left out has seen a similar increase from 2018 (52%, up from 47%)."[19]

- "The number of teens who get together with their friends nearly every day dropped by more than 40 percent from 2000 to 2015."[20]
- "Those whose jobs may inherently limit daily personal interaction—research, remote workers, clinical workers, and out-of office sales—all report higher levels of loneliness, along with skilled labor workers and those in the service industry."[21]

These statistics are hard to swallow. I know they were for me. But now you can see why I'm so committed to bringing this conversation to the masses.

We have to do something, right? These are our parents and siblings, our partners and children, and our friends and colleagues we are talking about.

The challenge before all of us is to face these hard truths head on:

- We have been led to believe that touch is bad or shameful or too challenging to address.
- Strong regulations and imposed boundaries around touch have made

things worse not better, and the research is starting to uncover these trends.

- We are so afraid to touch each other that we are ignoring people in need.
- We are creating distance and separation between ourselves at work and in our volunteer and spiritual communities.
- We are losing the capacity to build trust and compassion in our families and communities.
- We are so overwhelmed with messages about how to avoid touching people, how they should not be touching us, whether certain touch is right or wrong and how *should* we feel about it and whether we should report it or not, that we are on the verge of a cultural collapse.

The Remedy

Humans need to feel safe and like we belong or we can lose access to the parts of our brain that regulate mood, impulses, and behavior. If touch is one of the most simple, primal, and effective ways to make us feel both safe and loved; then why don't we, as a culture, change the messaging? Why don't we start talking about intention and safety, about consent and communication, and about how to bring healthy touch back into our individual lives, workplaces, and communities? Why don't we commit to taking personal responsibility for asking for what we need, asking for permission, and saying *no* when we need to instead of defaulting all of that responsibility to systems and organizations and their policy makers?

The purpose of this book is to start a new, healthier conversation (and a healing process) around the topic of touch for individuals and our culture. After my own journey, it is clear that this cultural transformation has to be grassroots. No general policies or rules for a culture (even a workplace) can make it as safe and healthy as it would be if each of us took personal responsibility for our own touch experience and then learned how to share it in healthy ways with others in every environment.

It's also important to note that the scope of this book is non-sexual touch. Sexual harassment education has helped many people and shed light on a serious problem. The #MeToo movement was powerful and brought forward important issues around touch and harassment, power differentials, abuse, and trauma.

Similarly, the LGBT+ movement has brought awareness of various relationships and identities in our culture. In this book, we will use men/women and he/she for simplicity of reading, but the content is meant to be inclusive of all no matter how you identify. These are important subjects and have shaped our current touch communities. Now is the time to harness the consent culture as well as people's desires to connect beyond social media and cell phones and bring back touch that heals, nourishes, and bonds.

I've designed this book to take courageous individuals like you on a personal journey around touch, so that you can cultivate healthy touch and improved well-being for yourself physically, in your relationships, and in the communities and systems in which you work and serve.

How to Get the Most Out of This Book

The reality is that we have been listening to and experiencing the impact of certain messages about touch since we were little; and the stories, lessons, and even the research I am about to share with you will challenge all of that. That means you will likely find yourself surprised or even upset by what you experience in this book.

In addition to my personal journey through touch challenges in my life, you will find research and studies that support bringing healthy, consensual touch into your life and your community. You will see me using some of the healing tools and modalities that I've used and that I share with my clients, and you will see some of my own mistakes and fears so you will know you are not alone when you feel challenged. You will also see how other people I know and have interviewed interact with touch so you can lean into what fits for you and your lifestyle, as well as have a broader cultural and global understanding around touch. Finally, there are a couple of questions at the end of each chapter to help guide you, and if you want to go deeper, you can find a series of deeper exercises to support you through each step at the end of the book ("Play & Explore"). Then, jump onto the TouchRemedies.com website to find support and additional opportunities for exploration through classes, workshops, or retreats.

When You Start to Feel

This book may bring up big emotions for you, and there is no right or wrong way to feel about physical touch. If you are a person who really enjoys touch and is frustrated by a culture that makes it tough for you to be real, you may experience more of that frustration as you read through my experiences. Some of you are touch-forward and are feeling confused and scared because the touch you gave so freely before seems like it can get you into trouble now, and you are not sure what to do about it. If you are someone who is touch-averse, you will likely find yourself resisting certain parts of this book. You may be touch-averse because you have had a challenging relationship to touch; you have grown up in a situation where touch was not part of your childhood or where physical contact was forbidden, dangerous, or shameful; or you have experienced a trauma or event that shaped your relationship to touch.

Touch challenges and traumas can take many forms, including the following:

- Physical boundaries not being honored
- Being forced to hug people you are uncomfortable with

- Over-enthusiastic hugs that hurt or made you feel trapped
- Pain or overstimulation when you are touched
- Any time you felt you could not protect yourself from being touched
- Having to give touch (even "good touch") to others who have sucked your energy
- Not knowing how to tell someone you are uncomfortable with their touch
- Getting a massage, physical therapy, or medical intervention that was uncomfortable
- Being tickled too much
- Having a medical procedure when young
- Being hit, slapped, or spanked
- Not being touched at all
- Withholding of touch as punishment
- Sexual molestation or rape
- Being shamed around touch
- Observing others experiencing touch violations
- Tolerating others' touch demands

For others, touch may be so foreign that you have to consciously make an effort to remember to hug or touch your partners and children and are a little sensitive when someone offers it. I find that a lot of touch-sensitive people are so because they don't interact with touch much or are empathic, so it feels overwhelming to the system. If you are touch-averse or touch-sensitive, you may even find yourself judging me for my actions or triggered by my words as your brain tries to keep you safe from the challenges posed by my experiences and suggestions.

If you choose more touch in your life, there are many resources and opportunities to encourage this growth in yourself and the people around you. No matter what your experience, I invite you to continue reading, even if you find yourself experiencing big feelings. Remember the following as you read:

1. **Take care of yourself** by setting your intention, creating your own sense of safety, and using self-care tools such as grounding, breathing, or journaling.

2. **Approach this new conversation with a child-like curiosity** about how you can integrate these concepts, tools, and suggestions into your life in a way that feels good for you.

3. **Find someone to talk to,** whether that is your personal support system, a therapist (especially if you've suffered touch trauma), or on the Touch Remedies page.

4. **Look into yourself and focus on personal healing** before you try to take this to a system, community, or culture.

> If it becomes too tough, there is a more detailed description of what you can do as well as a list of resources at the back of the book.

Remember the outcome will not look the same for everyone. This book is designed to take people on a personal journey. Some people just don't want to give or receive physical contact.

From anyone.

End of story.

Let me be really clear for those that choose "no-touch" after doing their own work around their history, wants, and needs. That choice is just as powerful as the choice to incorporate touch with everyone possible. Some of you are thinking "WHAT?? This is a book on touch. Isn't the point of this book to teach everyone to be touchy-feely and smile and touch and hug everyone and bounce around on rainbows?" Nope. This book is as much about finding your own clear and safe *no* around touch as much as it is encouraging you to reach out and ask for your *yes*.

It's clear that transforming *The Touch Crisis* needs to be a grassroots effort. No regulation can make it as safe and comprehensive as each of us taking responsibility for our own touch boundaries. No policy is going to educate us or our children to communicate our wants and needs. If we do not teach them to communicate when they are young, what will their touch future look like when people try to touch them in a way that is not comfortable? Will they just report it without an attempt at protecting themselves? Will they feel violated and hide? Or will they choose to stand up firmly and redirect to appropriate touch?

This endeavor to bring healthy touch back into our culture is a big one, and it is not for the faint of heart. My hope is this book will bring you one step closer to healing your own relationship with touch, so you will be able to enjoy more of it with family and friends and start to see how you can bring it into your life in a larger way to help us end *The Touch Crisis*.

BREAKING NEWS: COVID-19

"The governor has signed into effect Emergency Executive Order 20-20 today, directing Minnesotans to stay at home in response to the COVID-19 pandemic."

Of all the challenges that I anticipated and mentally prepared to address while getting ready to release this book, a pandemic that encouraged (and eventually forced) people to stay locked inside their homes for weeks (and eventually months) at a time was not on my radar. While people struggled with concepts of basic survival and navigated multiple opinions and regulations regarding physical interaction, I began reworking the speaking engagements I had booked to discuss bringing healthy touch into communities as an online experience, and I wondered how these newly-coined concepts of social and physical distancing were going to affect us as humans.

It was only a matter of weeks before I began to cringe at the long-term implications while watching the news and talking to friends and feeling the impact in my own body and psyche.

As fear swept across the world and people donned masks, all of our touch boundaries were challenged and changed. The reality of social distancing became more obvious and painful to touch-forward folks like myself, while some of our touch-sensitive friends took a collective sigh of relief. Some people are getting more touch than ever before as kids climb onto their laps during work meetings, their teens tap their shoulder to ask for attention at all times of the day, or their significant others demand consolation and connection. For them it feels there is no escape or way to ask for the break they need. On the other end of the spectrum many are completely alone, without even a furry snuggle to boost hormone levels. Many of my friends in this situation have shared with me the level of depression, the depths of their loneliness, and the touch starvation that is occurring, even among the most introverted. One of my friends, who lives mostly in isolation and has for many years, commented that now he does not even get the little touches from someone handing him change at the grocery store or the monthly breakfast with a friend. He is feeling the impact of the loss.

But then physical distancing became social isolation, as many stopped even saying "hello" while out on neighborhood walks or in the store, as if the mere acknowledgement of another human might infect or kill them.

This is not good, my friends.

At the time of printing no one knows what's going to happen, but I am extremely concerned for our culture and our mental/emotional and physical health—and not just because there is a strange virus sweeping the globe. In addition to the fact that many health professionals assert we need to engage in non-sterile environments to keep our immune systems strong, you will see, through this book, all of the research I have found that shows just how important touch is for our physical well-being as well as mental/emotional health.

Whether you are touch-forward, touch-averse, or touch-sensitive, long-term physical distancing is bad news for all of us.

We have no idea how people will want to interact as restrictions release or how the already culturally-taboo concept of physical touch will be regulated, restricted, feared, or embraced. However, I cannot think of a better time for us to all begin talking about how we can bring healthy physical contact back into our lives and communities.

All that said, this will likely change how you will read this book, which was moving into production just as the pandemic began.

In chapter one, where I address our well-worn touch patterns, you might realize that you are currently feeling differently about touch than you did before this pandemic. If that's true, take note of the differences. When you read about the importance of safety and intention in chapter two, I am well-aware that there will be another level of conversation happening around safety because of this pandemic. In chapter three you may shake your head at the thought of asking someone for a hug and replace it with physical contact that is perceived safer: "Would you like an elbow bump or a handshake?"

As you read, reflect not only how it was for you pre-COVID, but how you would like to embrace physical contact as we open our doors for connection and business once again.

On the other side of this pandemic, we may have to differentiate potential disadvantages versus advantages to touch. Are we not allowed to/supposed to, or are we just fearful of it? When we choose to touch, how could it be favorable or healthy for us? For example, I hugged a friend in a parking lot after a properly-distanced walk because she was so desperate for touch (as was I). As I hugged her I saw the looks others gave us: some neutral, some shaming. I wanted to scream, "Don't you know that hugs are very good for our immune system?" Instead, I closed my eyes and focused on the love and health and positive intent I had for my completely isolated friend.

I have read articles stating that social distancing is here to stay, and others stating that the increased level of depression and loneliness is augmented by "skin hunger," a basic human need for physical contact. Other discussions revolve around how even handshakes should become taboo in the name of public safety. It seems many people do not know touch itself boosts immunity and makes us more resilient to illness.

The good news is that you and I can begin to have discussions on how vital touch is going to be to become reconnected, to boost our immune systems, and to find a modicum of normalcy in a world that seems turned upside-down.

We can do this together!

"If you change the way you look at things, the things you look at change."

~ Wayne Dyer, American self-development speaker and author ~

CHAPTER 1
RUTS & REMEDIES
Scouting Your Inner Terrain

Unknown Territory

"I've got my bags," I texted Sofia as I walked out of the airport into the evening air, more exhausted from my travel than I had anticipated.

They were waiting at the curb. "Hi! Welcome home," she said. I crouched to match her height and she wrapped me up in a warm full-body hug, her long dark hair brushing against my hands. "Let me grab that for you." She reached for my bag and began piling my stuff into the car as I turned to Lance.

"Hi Dear, it's so good to see you." He opened his arms and I stepped into the warm welcome.

It is so great to see them, I thought as I climbed into the car, glad to have such a soft landing after nine months on the road. *It feels really surreal to be back. Hmmm.*

Back—not home. That's interesting, I observed as I settled in for the forty-minute drive back to their place where I would be staying for a few days.

"Are you hungry? Do you want to go out and grab food?" Lance inquired from behind the driver's seat, looking over his shoulder to pull out of the busy terminal.

"Or we have food at home if you would prefer." Sofia chimed in. "We weren't sure how hungry you would be or how tired. It's completely up to you."

"Hmmm...." I thought for a bit before responding. I really wanted to go out and be in the activity and comfort of a local restaurant, but I could feel my body protesting at the thought. *It's midnight. Do you really need to go out and eat?*

My mind responded to my body, *You need to reset your timing anyway. May as well go out and enjoy the company of friends and the activity of the city.*

"Nah." My body won. "It would be good to get settled in and move a bit. I've been sitting too long."

They asked me about my flight, how I was feeling, and how I envisioned the next couple of days together. Both of them assured me they wanted nothing more than for me to be cozy and comfortable and to feel nurtured and loved.

Man, I have such great people in my life, I marveled. *I can't imagine an easier way to return to my life here, especially after all the personal disconnects in the last few months.*

When we arrived at their place, I dumped my stuff in the guest bedroom and glanced at myself in the full-length mirror to see if I looked as tired as I felt. My green eyes looked bright, the lines around them deep from years of adventure and laughter. The months of hiking had tanned my Scandinavian skin, lightened my loosely-braided blonde hair, and kept my 5'8" frame toned. Toting around that fifty-pound rucksack was a great workout even when I wasn't hiking.

Time to change, I thought as I looked at my long flowing cotton massage pants, hiking tank top, and warm North Face fleece I was wearing. I changed into yoga pants and a t-shirt to get more cozy, walked to the living room, and flopped down on the couch where they were already seated. This easy, comfortable connection was reminding me of a couple incidents in the UK, and I had to update them on my perspectives of cultural differences in dating.

"So... after being on the road for seven months and doing a meditation retreat where we weren't allowed to touch anyone for ten days, I went hiking on the Cotswold Way in England. They have this amazing pub there," I started, loving the fact that I was in a safe space and could talk as loudly as I wanted and use as many hand gestures as I could without standing out. "And I ended up chatting with a group of locals and got invited to hang out at their table."

"No surprise there," joked Sofia, who fondly calls me her one extroverted friend.

I grinned and continued. "Anyway, I ended up being asked out by this guy, Eric, who was pretty cute, and a bit taller than me. He seemed intelligent and respectful, so I accepted."

"We went out a few times," I continued, gaining pace and volume as I felt the warmth of the memory and the excitement of the evenings return. "The first time we hung out, he was talking about his daughter and kept touching my arm while he talked. It felt really natural and comfortable, and I felt really connected to him. The next time we went to a fun English Pub down the street from the first place. He seemed super interested, and was really touchy for a Brit; but respectfully so." I had learned from being in England a few times that people touch a lot less than they do even in the U.S.

"So then we decide to do dinner a third night. And this is what is so weird," I said, already feeling my body tighten and my stomach flip at the memory of the confusing signals.

"Eric said he was exhausted when he picked me up, and acted a little off all night. He barely ate anything, and it was challenging to get him to talk at all. I thought maybe I had done or said something wrong, but as we left the restaurant he grabbed my hand and held it all the way back to the car." I paused, remembering how that little bit of touch felt like an acknowledgment that we were still connected and not to be concerned. "So we made plans to meet up again."

"Then, the day he's supposed to meet me, he texts me saying he got into a fender-bender the night before so couldn't. But still wondering about the mixed signals from the previous time, I called him. He was super nervous and couldn't answer my question directly. Then told me he'd call me back. Of course he didn't."

Who grabs and holds someone's hand and then texts a last-minute cancellation? Had I just been so lacking in touch that I misinterpreted him? And why the heck does it still feel so disappointing? And why is it making me so needy for touch right now?

"You did nothing wrong, my dear," Sofia reassured. "And who knows, he probably didn't know how to deal with the fact you would be coming back to the U.S." She let the possibility hang in the air for a moment. "Want to watch a show? We have this great show called *Very British Problems* that I think would explain this well."

I agreed and we moved to the lower level entertainment room, custom-made for movie watching with 3D sound. We cozied up together on the long, comfortable couch facing the TV, threw a soft blanket over us, and laughed our way through the rest of the evening until I finally complied with my body and drifted off into a deep sleep.

I woke up early the following day, and just laid in bed for a bit, analyzing my body and mind since I had my first full-day home ahead of me. *I'm feeling really comfortable and at peace. It's lovely how quickly I went from feeling an acute lack of touch to really feeling content and supported.*

Feeling energized, I bounced out of bed and wandered out to the computer room to meet my friends who were doing some work from home that day. After a round of morning hugs, we headed off to the kitchen for coffee and breakfast and to catch up on all the news of jobs, friends, and my plans for being home and returning to Europe.

It was all easy and relaxed until that afternoon.

I was ready to go for a walk. My legs felt tired, but the kind of tired you get when you haven't moved at all— that sluggish, apathetic, yet restless feeling that makes me have to really ask myself if I want to go to bed or get up and move.

The three of us stepped out the front door, and as Lance turned to make sure it was locked I felt a little pang of something in my chest. *Annoyance? Why on earth would I be annoyed? There is absolutely nothing wrong. Perhaps it's just the jet-lag.* I trusted the bright sun overhead and the crispness of the April air to settle me as I wandered along beside Lance and Sofia down the city street to the quieter paved bike path flanked by trees and parks.

What a beautiful day, I mused, still curious about this feeling in my chest. *I'm sure this feeling will subside as I move. I just got really used to hiking almost every* day so I'm sure two days of sitting is really taking a toll.* Unfortunately, the quiet discontent grew as we walked along. I looked at the bare trees and smelled the first bits of spring in the air, even as I analyzed the red sand from Texas that had arrived on a large storm and created a pattern in the remaining snow piles. *Are we walking too slowly? Have I gotten so used to walking in mountains and across fields that the city no longer offers any comfort?*

I tuned back into the conversation between Lance and Sofia and their plans for managing a couple of looming work projects. "Is there any way you can just not do all the work if you can't hire another assistant right away?" I volunteered, my mind only half into the conversation. I started to fidget as I walked, twisting my back and allowing my arms to follow the momentum and slap against my body before turning the other direction and repeating the process.

Sofia replied, "I mean, I could but the work has to get done on a deadline so either I do it now or later. I've asked for as much help as I can and have delegated other things. But seriously, if they don't get me help, I won't go through another six months like last time. I'll just quit. I already told my boss that as well."

Why do I feel so overwhelmed right now? I am in the most relaxed, safe, comfortable environment with two great friends. But I couldn't shake the feeling that there was too much input—that my body was in some kind of physical overwhelm or energetic crisis. I took a deep breath, hooked my arms behind my back, stretched out my neck, shook each leg around a bit, and continued to fidget as we walked back toward the house.

After a brief moment of stress where we thought we were locked out of the house, Lance managed to get the garage door open. We walked through the dark, narrow, tiled basement hallway single-file, the potential disaster averted but still hanging heavy in the air.

"Do you want some water or anything?" Sofia asked, touching my arm as we entered the kitchen from the basement.

Oh my gosh, please don't touch me. I was startled by my own internal reaction at such a small, innocuous and normal gesture. *What is going on with me?*

As soon as I asked the question, I got my answer. I had gone from barely any touch to loads of it in less than twenty-four hours. My internal need for touch had completely reset itself while I was in Europe, and I was full-up.

I didn't actually think it was possible for me to get too much touch, I mused, struck and semi-amused by the conflict of being so grateful and wanting to hug Sofia and Lance for all their hospitality while at the same time wanting to shut myself in a room and hide.

As I gulped down some water I applauded myself inwardly for making this connection. With this awareness, I knew that I could make a clear choice on how to interact with my friends for the rest of the day.

Yes, this is a far cry from a few years ago when I was struggling with how to negotiate physical contact with people I love, including my clients. I'm so glad my awareness has increased.

As Sofia and Lance busied themselves in the kitchen, I let my mind wander back to one day at work several months after being accused of acting unprofessional and inappropriate with touch.

Messy, Muddy Trails

After changing the sheets and cleaning the table from the previous massage client, I walked out into the open waiting room of my wellness center. My friend, Lisa, was sitting in the lounge chair patiently waiting, and I was feeling anxiety about greeting her. I always saw her both at business and at smaller, more intimate personal functions; but we hadn't really hung out together, *per se*, on our own as friends. *Should I offer a handshake? A hug like we do at personal events? Ask her to follow me as I lead her back to my room?* I shook my head at the thought that something that used to come so easily and naturally was suddenly a source of constant angst.

She jumped up as I walked toward her. "Oh my gosh, my shoulder is killing me! You have no idea how happy I am you could sneak me in for an appointment today!" she exclaimed, taking the lead and walking back to the massage room.

Well, that was easy, I thought as I followed her.

When the massage ended, I washed my hands and made my way to the front desk where my loyal receptionist and friend, Rebeccah, was working hard. I stood a pace behind her and pretended to watch her work while I stressed about what would happen when Lisa emerged from the room. *I'll just chat with her from back here, pass her off to Rebeccah, and head back to my room. Ugh.* I felt so disingenuous; so lost. *I would have stayed in front of the desk before and at least touched her on the arm or shoulder as I said "goodbye and thank you." Now I'm hiding back here like a chastised child.*

"Yes, Dawn?" Rebeccah said, sensing the intensity of my emotion and gaze over her shoulder.

"Oh, ummm, nothing. Just thinking," I replied, turning to the other computer and flopping into the chair to check my emails and keep myself distracted from the discomfort in my heart and the subtle layer of shame that had been plaguing me ever since that woman had cornered me on the street.

Have I really been inappropriate all these years? I wondered as I stared at the computer screen. *Ugh, and then that ethics class...* I recalled a chapter in a book that was under review where I taught massage at the technical college. It addressed how to greet clients and how to send them off in a way that keeps boundaries and clarity between the client/practitioner relationship. It emphasized that hugging was not appropriate, because it could confuse the client and create a boundary violation.

Those books really don't cover dual relationships well enough. They don't address at all what it's like to be in a small town where you have two different relationships with so many people. I bet I've interacted with at least 25% of my clients on a social basis, and at least 10% were friends or acquaintances first. If we are both comfortable hugging outside the office, can't I at least say hello or goodbye with a hug here as well? It feels so awkward and insincere not to offer. Especially with Lisa. She's pretty touchy with a lot of women, and I see her most Thursday nights at our gathering. Maybe she is the one that started hugs with me; and if I'm hiding back here, I could offend her through my disconnection.

Restless and frustrated, I stood up and smiled at Lisa as she came to the desk. After I thanked her cheerily, I walked back to the safety of my room to prepare for my next client. While I sanitized the table, I thought back to the first weeks after the "shaming incident."

So much pain and confusion, I remembered. *I analyzed every single hug and touch I had given, every single interaction with students, co-volunteers, businesspeople in town, and even some of my friends.* Conversations about it with my husband hadn't eased my fear or guilt, even as he assured me that I was pretty intuitive about others' touch boundaries and probably hadn't done anything wrong. *I wanted to believe him, and I guess my apology to Pete confirmed it a bit.*

Pete had been a friend for about a year by the time this incident transpired. Our connection was easy, and we had crossed paths many times at business events and on the streets while heading to meetings at opposite ends of town. Most of these quick conversations ended with a hug.

I never thought anything about it before she chastised me on the street. Then I felt terrible, thinking I may have offended him.

As I finished wiping down the table and setting the room, I recalled the intense concern and confusion on his face when I apologized to him for these quick goodbye hugs we'd shared every time we'd finished a good conversation. He'd told me he'd taken no offense, and while that had lightened my burden of fear, I walked away from that moment feeling disconnected and disingenuous.

And of course, that created a level of awkwardness in our relationship.

I opened the door, took a deep breath, and went out to meet my next client; the question of how to greet them still heavy in my mind.

Muddy Boots: Why'd I bring it with me?

My poor clients and colleagues! I'm sure many of them wondered why I stopped hugging them. I shook my head to myself and turned my attention back to the friends in front of me. As Sofia refilled my glass with more water, Lance touched my arm, "Excuse me, Dear. I'm going to sneak by you and grab more coffee from the pantry."

Geez. I was suddenly aware of each little touch in a way I had never been before. I skootched closer to the counter as he slipped by me, hand on my arm the whole time.

I hear about moms being overwhelmed with touch all the time. It must be like this for them—times a thousand! At least I don't have anyone clinging to me, and I can go to the bathroom alone. I giggled to myself, trying to take a sip from my glass.

"What's so funny?" Sofia asked, looking puzzled.

I shrugged and smiled. "Oh, I'm just thinking about a few things. No big deal." I didn't want to share about my "touch overwhelm" and risk having them not touch me at all—or even worse, hurt their feelings or have them feel rejected.

Lance snuck by me again, once again touching my shoulder to let me know he was behind me. I looked over my shoulder and grinned as he went by, and he returned the smile.

"I'm really glad to be here with the two of you," I said, genuinely feeling the gratitude and warmth in my heart. "Thank you so much for taking such good care of me."

"You are always welcome here," Lance said.

"Yeah, and you help us actually get out and go for walks like we always intend when we work from home," Sofia grinned. "It's fun to have your energy around. Plus, you get my brain." We shared a laugh as Lance started the coffee grinder, thus driving us into the living room to seek a bit of insulation from the noise.

"What else is happening?" I asked Sofia, as we snuggled into the soft, warm couch.

"Well, I think you are caught up on all the basics," she said. "Anything else you want to chat about?"

"Not really," I said, thinking about all the stories I still hadn't told but wasn't really in the mood to tell. "I mean, I could talk for hours, but I'm feeling like I should probably check my work emails and make sure I'm all set for my clients in a couple days."

"Yeah," Sofia said, "we technically have the day off but you know how that goes around here." She shrugged and stood up. "There are a few 'must-do' things today for each of us." She met Lance at the kitchen doorway and gave him the update, "Hon, I'm going to get a bit of work done so I don't have to think about it."

They shared a quick kiss before Lance came over to where I was sitting on the end of the couch and gave my shoulder a few squeezes with his free hand.

How can that feel so great and too much at the same time? I wondered as my body cheered, *YES! Don't stop—my shoulders are so tight.*

"Do you mind if I go work for a bit, too? That will give us freedom after dinner."

"Please, go ahead," I said. "I have lots I should be doing as well."

Lance headed off, the smell of his latte lingering in the air. I grabbed my laptop and sat up straighter, crossing my legs and getting ready to do some real work.

I stared at the screen and resisted opening social media as my mind started wandering. I thought about how Sofia and Lance interacted so easily with touch, and then thought about my marriage.

We were so good at using touch with each other in day-to-day interactions, I remembered and smiled, as I felt my heart open. We had both read the book *The 5 Love Languages*, and realized that our main language was touch, which meant we both felt loved when we received touch.

Sure doesn't feel like touch is my love language right now, I thought, *or is it possible that touch sensitivity and need falls on a spectrum? Maybe we can be conditioned to be comfortable with it and need it; but when we are lacking, our bodies become more sensitive to it?*

I pondered this thought as my brain brought up examples of people in different audiences who had shared with me that they didn't like to be touched—massage students, teachers, men and women of all backgrounds, ages, and upbringings. Even a couple of clients who were forced to come in for a session by their loved one. Finally, my thoughts turned to Diane, who had asked me not to touch her or her boyfriend—and the woman who had shamed me for hugging everyone after receiving my award.

I know some people are sensitive because of past traumas, but I wonder if others dislike touch because they feel overwhelmed by the sensations. Maybe it's not part of their everyday lives the way it wasn't part of mine in Europe. That would be so sad, I thought as I turned my attention back to my computer. *I'm glad this hasn't been the case for me.*

My First Footprints

I grew up in a family that showed a lot of affection, and it was normal to give and receive several hugs a day. Even my grandparents were affectionate. My dad's father had lost his leg in an accident before I was born, and so I grew up with the luxury of sitting on his wooden leg and giving a hug whenever I wanted that little bit of childlike closeness—even into my twenties. It wasn't until years after his death that my mom had mentioned that when she first came into the family, Grandpa did not hug. But, having had a very affectionate mother herself, she would say, "I love you," and give him and my grandmother a hug, until everyone became not only conditioned to hugs, but enjoyed and initiated touch. By the time I was born it was something so natural that I never would have guessed anything different. That's why I was surprised when I went to college and began to realize that some people were so deprived of touch that there was a whole community and industry geared around using touch for healing.

I was introduced to this concept by my friend Chris when I was nineteen years old and starting my second year at the university. When he had told me he was going to be a massage therapist for a living, I actually asked, "Is that really a career?" I was clearly conditioned to believe I had to graduate from a university to be successful, but I was intrigued as he told me about a modality called Therapeutic Touch he was learning through the nurses on campus. He asked if I wanted to meet them and learn the technique.

I did. That day changed my life.

I could immediately feel changes in my body, and I was hooked. I met with them almost every Wednesday and took further training on complimentary medicine approaches the following semester, as well as the first two levels of Therapeutic Touch on the weekends. At the end of the year, I'd made the choice to leave the university to attend massage school in Salt Lake City.

Off the Map

Staring at my computer screen, I was thoroughly restless and engrossed in my thoughts. *It's amazing that I never questioned the power of a hug until I was shamed for it. That really shifted the core of how I interact with the world.*

I cringed again as I remembered that experience with Lisa and other clients, and Pete's confused expression when I apologized.

A sudden heaviness filled my chest.

Dawn, you didn't know then what you know now, I reminded myself. *Everything you were taught about touch boundaries as a child and in school revolved around staying away from sexual touch. And because you were a touchy person, you hung out with other touchy people.*

Except Diane, the critical voice inside me said, *if you had learned more quickly from that, you could have avoided everything else.*

I contemplated that for a moment, using my tools to be gentle with myself about my past learning experiences.

You did learn from that. You learned to be more aware of how you hug people, and would ask sometimes if people were up for a hug. You just didn't realize people also didn't always say no when they meant it, or that outside people could get offended by your actions. Remember, that's why you went to the Hoffman Process.

Very Old Ruts

Fortunately for me, I had been working monthly with a homeopath for years before the "shaming incident" had happened. I believe strongly that to be a good practitioner of any healing modality, we should be doing our own healing so we can be better for our clients.

While I was considering divorce, he told me that he believed in order for me to get to the next level of my healing journey I needed to become more aware of the root of my thoughts, feelings, behaviors, and overall patterns. He recommended the Hoffman Process, which is a week-long retreat in which you identify negative ways of thinking and being that developed unconsciously through childhood conditioning. We all have been conditioned from the time we are very young. From infancy until we are around six years old, our brains run on delta and theta waves, which means that what we see and perceive gets downloaded directly into our subconscious. Our young brains, acting like sponges, create stories based on personal experience, observed behaviors of those around us, adult messaging, and cultural and social cues that subconsciously inform how we will interact with the world for the rest of our lives—until we bring awareness to them. Think of them as patterns or habits of "being" that can become our default reactions. Once you have awareness, you get to make aligned choices in your life instead of blindly reacting and defaulting to habit.

The process was amazing, and I learned a lot about myself and the underlying causes for both my actions and emotional responses. I also uncovered how I would distract myself with exercise, music, or activity to avoid feeling emotions when things were tough. When that stopped being effective, I would find ways to numb; whether through books, over-working, cooking, drinking, or complete avoidance.

I realized at Hoffman that touch was the thing that would bring me back from the feelings of numbness and apathy, and it was the way that I felt connected to people in general. Touch was key in my method for feeling accepted and acknowledged. Since that was a lesson I absorbed when I was young, it became crystal clear to me that by making the choice to process and work with emotions, my touch would come from a place of choice and intention and would be more powerful both for me and for anyone receiving touch from me.

Not only did the process teach me a lot about myself, it also showed me that other people's actions are not always conscious or clear—that we all often live from a place of compulsion, habit, or belief we have never analyzed; even if it does not feel exactly right for us. It also taught me that through self-exploration and healing, each of us is able to make different choices and have different reactions to anything. From that understanding, I was able to come from a much deeper level of compassion and empathy for others on touch and other topics.

Even though the "shaming incident" shook me to my core and had me, once again, question everything I believed in, I was grateful that it brought my awareness back to the arena of touch; I was able to truly explore what it meant to touch and to be touched, and how it could be done in a respectful and conscious manner, no matter what the other's background is.

Finding My Way Back to the Trail

Yes, that was one of the best things I ever did for myself, I thought as I opened up my email. *That awareness and self-knowledge has served me well over the years, and it is absolutely allowing me to make healthy choices, rather than revert to old patterns while I'm feeling so touch-sensitive around these dear friends. Go, me!* I cheered and then dove headfirst into a few hours of administrative tasks to prepare for the weeks of work ahead.

Remedies
The Open Prairie

Without awareness and self-knowledge, we are simply mimicking the patterns we learned in our environment. For the sake of this book, I want to focus on both the patterns and potential around touch.

We are living in a culture where tactile communication, a.k.a. touch, has become more taboo as the fear around how we should and should not touch each other has grown. No-touch policies have been instituted in schools and workplaces, while policies and regulations have been tightened in others, including a variety of healing professions ranging from medical doctors to psychotherapists to massage therapists.

The #MeToo movement, although important for awareness and for women (and men) to finally speak their truth and receive support, has escalated the fear of touching others to the point that my dad overheard a woman at a playground refuse to help a child in need: "I'm not touching someone else's kid." Our fear of lawsuits and sexual harassment allegations have tipped us past the point of clear communication and healthy social interactions and into a forced personal seclusion that separates us from each other and our communities.

Restricting touch is not as healthy for our culture as it first seems. A position statement by the National

Association for the Education of Young Children (NAEYC) states:

6. Programs should not institute "no-touch policies" to reduce the risk of abuse... No-touch policies are misguided efforts that fail to recognize the importance of touch to children's healthy development. Touch is especially important for infants and toddlers. Warm, responsive touches convey regard and concern for children of any age. Adults should be sensitive to ensuring that their touches (such as pats on the back, hugs, or ruffling the child's hair) are welcomed by the children and appropriate to their individual characteristics and cultural experience. Careful, open communication between the program and families about the value of touch in children's development can help to achieve consensus as to acceptable ways for adults to show their respect and support for children in the program.[22]

I love this statement because it not only addresses the need for touch, but for the personal and cultural sensitivity and the communication needed to experience it in a healthy way. We have known from studies by René Spitz in the 1940s and 50s, from the Bucharest Early Intervention Project in this century, and from studies done with premature infants that touch is vitally important for brain development, physical and mental growth, and immunity.

Touch is not only important for infants though. Children of all ages need touch. Studies show when kids roughhouse it stimulates a chemical in the brain (BDNF) that improves memory and learning capabilities, and they have more positive feeling about themselves.[23] Touch has been shown to decrease aggressive tendencies in our youth. Andrew W. Prescott was one of the first to document the correlation between the amount of physical affection children received as infants from their mother and the propensity toward violence in the culture.[24] Tiffany Field, the director of the Touch Research Institute, found that European adolescents received more affectionate touch than their United States counterparts, which is reflected in the increased aggression in the U.S. youth.[25]

But that does not mean we outgrow the need for touch when we become adults. Touch has been shown to reduce stress, heart-rate, and blood pressure. A variety of studies point to the willingness of adult strangers, colleagues, and teams to work more closely when touch is integrated. A study done by Nicolas Guéguen showed that if a professor gave a slight tap on the upper arm while giving verbal encouragement to his students who were volunteering to solve a problem on the board, they were more 19% more likely to volunteer again than those who were not touched.[26] Doctors who touch their patients often are perceived as more caring. A study on touch behaviors in the National Basketball Association "confirmed that touch predicted improved performance even after accounting for player status, preseason expectations, and early season performance."[27] In other words, the more often a team touched in their preseason, the better they did—which has larger implications for other group and team settings, including in the workplace.

The physical science supports this, showing how touch and hugs release the hormone, oxytocin, also sometimes called the "cuddling hormone." Oxytocin has been found to increase trust in social interactions, increase social bonding, decrease sensitivity to social exclusion, and foster generosity. One study administered oxytocin or placebo to sixty participants and found that participants who had taken oxytocin were forty-four times more trusting that their privacy would not be violated than participants on placebo.[28] Another showed that it increased ratings of trustworthiness relative to control ratings in both genders. One study on oxytocin and team sports says, "It is a critical neuropeptide involved in shaping of important team processes in sport such as trust, generosity, altruism, cohesion, cooperation, and social motivation."[29]

I don't want to gloss over the fact that there is emerging research showing that oxytocin is not as impactful on people who have experienced "high levels of parental-love withdrawal,"[30] or that some people are more touch-sensitive than others. However, according to psychologist Matthew Hertenstein, PhD, director of the Touch and Emotion Lab at DePauw University, touch deprivation is a real thing. "Most of us, whatever our relationship status, need more human contact than we're getting. Compared with other cultures, we live in a touch-phobic society that's made affection with anyone but loved ones taboo."[31]

Did You Know?

"A child's perceptions of the world are directly downloaded into the subconscious during [the first six years of life], without discrimination and without filters of the analytical self-conscious mind which doesn't fully exist. Consequently, our fundamental perceptions about life and our role in it are learned without our having the capacity to choose or reject those beliefs. We were simply programmed."[32]

Marion Diamond, a professor of anatomy at the University of California at Berkeley, showed that rats who had more tactile experience had better-developed nerve cells in the area of the cortex that processes the sensations of touch. "People who touch little, as opposed to those who like to cuddle, probably experience the same effect. Those who have had little physical contact over the years might become hypersensitive to such touch, so that they found it physically uncomfortable.'"[33]

"'When you're being touched by another person, your brain isn't set up to give you the objective qualities of that touch,' says Michael Spezio, coauthor of a 2012 study on how parts of the brain (specifically primary somatosensory cortices) interpret touch.

> **'The entire experience is affected by your social evaluation of the person touching you.'**[34]
>
> Pleasant touch, including physical contact with an animal, not only increases oxytocin, it also increases other hormones such as the natural antidepressant serotonin and the pleasure chemical dopamine. When these hormones are balanced, you can experience a stronger immune response, an improved mood, and less inflammation.

An Internal Peek

Most of us need more touch, and the science shows us why. The challenge is that, like me before the Hoffman Process and the "shaming incident", most of us don't really take the time to think about our experience with touch.

What are the touch trails that led you to this book? If you could make one change in your touch habits, beliefs, or interactions, what would it be?

For a more detailed exploration of your touch trails, I invite you to turn to the "Play and Explore" section for chapter one in the back of this book.

"Fear is a question.
What are you afraid of and why?
Our fears are a treasure house of self-knowledge if we explore them."

~ Marilyn French,
Author and feminist activist ~

CHAPTER 2
ROUTES & RESOURCES
Strategizing Your Intention and Safety

A Familiar Start

I had been back from Europe for about six weeks and was living with my parents. Having sold my house before I left the first time, there was not enough time between my trips to justify renting a different space.

It's so interesting to be back in a routine with my parents, I thought as I sat on the edge of my childhood bed and looked around my childhood room. *So familiar yet so different at the same time. I guess we've all changed.* I gazed out the window that overlooked the back hill and the large forest I used to explore with my dog, Ben. Hiding behind the new sheer white curtains were the blackout shades I remembered as a child. *I'm amazed we have these so deep in the country, but they are necessary for those long days.* The walls and carpet were still the pink-peach color I chose when I was young, and my clunky oak desk and bright red chair were still there; piled high with books, unopened mail, and my in-progress client cases. My posters had been replaced with pictures, and the open folding doors of the closet revealed my mother's clothes instead of mine. The dark dresser and nightstand were new additions, as well as the ceiling fan above me.

Sitting opposite from the door that led down the hall to the rest of the house, I smiled as I watched my mom scurry out from the bathroom where she had just taken her shower, dash down the hallway, and turn into the living room. *Probably heading to the kitchen to figure out where she lost her coffee this time,* I thought with amusement. *Some things never change.*

My first few weeks had been complete chaos as I caught up on clients at both offices, spent time with friends, and settled into the rhythm of being back in the U.S.

Thank goodness my parents were still in Florida when I arrived. I didn't have to navigate so many changes at once and could get into my own rhythm here. But for some reason, I'm still not feeling really connected with them. It's probably because I haven't been home while they are awake, except for in the mornings when we are all in our morning routines. The realization came with a bit of guilt and sadness. Some of the loneliness I thought had left me over the last few weeks suddenly washed over my body and into my chest, leaving me feeling empty and needy.

I looked at my watch and began picking up all of the items I'd organized on the dresser. *I better get going. I want a bit of time to chat with them before I go to work and I don't want to be late. Laptop, keys, wallet, phone. I already took my sheets to the car with my lunch. I'm good to go.* I walked down the hall, through the living room into the adjoined dining room and kitchen, where my dad was busy cooking himself eggs and toast.

My goodness, that's loud. The newscaster's melodramatic voice was spouting off the latest news. *I wish he'd wear his hearing aids in the morning. Or turn on music instead. Maybe I should do that for him? It puts us all in a better mood anyway.* The jarring sound was a sharp contrast to the depth of longing I felt inside. *I really need a good hug.*

"Hey, Honey," my dad greeted me, looking over the counter where he was waiting for his toast. "Heading to work already?"

"Yep. Another full day of clients. I should be home early tonight though, around 9 p.m. or so," I responded, leaning back against the double oven across from him. I looked around the long, narrow space that hadn't changed since I was little, and then out the windows that overlooked the birdfeeders and front lawn. My mom was nowhere in sight. *She must have run to the basement office to check emails.*

"Well, I should still be up. I've got to mow the lawn a bit today, then see if I can figure out how to hit that ball on the golf course. My game has just sucked lately." He shook his head as he buttered the freshly-popped toast and turned to the stove to get his eggs.

"It's because you get too stressed about it," I joked. "Look at me, I only play a couple times a year and I'm great at it!" Our tradition together was to not keep score when we played, so all of my good rounds were top-of-mind.

I set my laptop down on the beige tile floor so I could give him a hug before I left. My need for touch had returned during the last few weeks. *It didn't take me long to get over my touch sensitivity,* I mused, thinking of all the hugs with family, clients, and friends in the last month. *Luckily, I'm in the right spot for a really good one before heading to work.*

Plate in hand, my dad reached his other arm out and gave me a quick squeeze. "Have a great day at work, Honey. It will be nice to see you when you get home tonight," he finished, walking over to pick up his coffee cup.

Is that it? I thought, suddenly panicked and dissatisfied. *Give me a real hug, dammit! Stop being in your routine and pay attention to ME!!* The child in me screamed, remembering those long, comforting hugs I got when I was little—when he'd wrap me up in comfort and love—the kind that made my body feel snuggly and safe.

You are an adult now, my mind reminded me. *You're not supposed to need that kind of attention from your parents.* I felt the familiar surge of unmet emotions rising into my throat. It felt like I wanted to throw a mini-tantrum to release the emotional void that I could feel growing deep in my stomach.

Come on! Logic battled with my emotions, *You are living in their house for free, eating their food, and they have offered you support for whatever you need to be successful. This knowledge should be enough. Stop being a child and get to work.*

"You too, Dad," I replied, lost in my internal battle. I walked over and grabbed a banana off the counter to fill the emptiness in my center. "I look forward to talking tonight. Maybe a game of cribbage?"

Some kind of connection beyond sitting and talking while you both watch tv? I kept my frustration-fueled sarcasm to myself.

"We'll see. Depends on how tired I am." He wandered over to the table to eat.

"Okay." I turned and walked the couple of steps to the basement door. "BYE, MOM!" I yelled, suddenly not wanting to risk going to give her a hug and feeling a second round of disappointment.

"Have a good day! See you tonight?" She yelled loudly in return.

"YEP!" I grabbed my laptop, turned, and walked out the front door to my car, completely unsatisfied, but completely adult.

As I drove the familiar streets, feeling the sadness grow in my chest, I realized that I would have to be far more intentional about asking for the type of touch I needed.

These are just old patterns, I assured myself. *I know I have the ability to start over and create new ones. Heaven knows I've done it before.*

I smiled as I reflected on the outcome of setting new intentions for my business almost four years before, even though there were some serious bumps along the way because of that "shaming incident."

New Trails in Friendly Territory

New location, new intentions, I affirmed as I stood outside the two-story wooden building near my hometown of Stillwater. I had sold my large business in Red Wing so I could focus on growing the non-deep-tissue massage part of my practice, opened a one-room space for myself in the same area, and now stood in front of my newly-opened second location inside a salon. *This business is going to focus on the emotional support and the mind-body connection. Massage is going to play a part, but not the lead. Especially the deep stuff. Eighteen years is a long time to use my body so hard.*

I'd chosen this location not only for the proximity to the people I knew in the Twin Cities; but because Angela, the owner, was familiar with homeopathy and excited to see that kind of complementary practice added to her facility. *Most people don't even know what homeopathy and CranioSacral are, not to mention having potential referral sources for me.*

I walked into the salon looking like a pack mule with my linens, food, and computer hanging off both sides. The warm wooden floors of the old building radiated comfort and style, yet also accentuated the modern glass shelves filled with hair and body products. I could smell the coffee as one of the receptionists walked by me to deliver a cup to a client. The front desk and open waiting room to my left was buzzing with activity.

"Okay, my dear," I noticed one of the stylists smile radiantly and step out from behind the front desk to give her client a giant hug before sending her off with a, "Looking forward to seeing you in six weeks."

I heard another stylist laugh loudly from her station on the other side of the salon, and glanced over to see her hand on her client's upper arm as they both giggled about whatever information was just shared.

Another stylist was enthusiastically welcoming her client seated near the desk, resting her hand easily on her arm and guiding her back to the station.

I love how synergistic and connected this place is. Angela really did a great job building the community here. I smiled and returned greetings as I made my way past the desk to the stairs that led to the quiet spa and wellness area. *They really reminded me how to be connected and offer touch to my clients again.* I felt appreciation warm my chest and expand my smile as I started my ascent. *It's just a part of the culture for us to touch each other, and that energy and comfort extends to the people that come here.*

Being new to this office, I was able to create different habits with my clients, coming around the desk to be close enough to touch, and allowing them to lead. I had noticed I would offer men handshakes instead of waiting, but allowed women to give some kind of body signal that they wanted touch.

I have seen a couple of my male clients hug their stylists. Perhaps I should just ask if they want a hug and start opening that possibility. Maybe it's time to open my intention and work more with my own hesitation and fear that I'll offend or they will misinterpret.

"Yep," I said out loud to myself as I walked back to my room, "it's really time to get over this and get back to being yourself!"

I opened the door to my room and set everything on the chair.

"Oh my goodness, look at the time,"[35] I said out loud, mimicking the clock voice from *Beauty and the Beast*. "Get your stuff set up and get downstairs. Your massage client is going to be here in a few minutes."

Feeling playful and high-energy, I prepped my room, scuttled down the stairs in my socks to the front desk, and greeted my client who had just arrived. "It's so nice to see you again!" I said enthusiastically, touching her on the arm, "Do you need the bathroom or water first? Or are you ready?"

"I'm all set." She smiled and I led her up the stairs to the room, where I went through the normal questions with her—asking about her response to the session last time, how it held, if she was sore, what she was looking for this time, and if she had any concerns. After her few quick answers, I left the room and returned when she indicated she was ready.

"Is this the pressure you are looking for?" I asked after about five minutes, noticing her eyes were now open and she was blankly staring off to the corner as I worked on her shoulder.

She seems distracted, but something about her energy isn't the same as usual. Like she wants something different she hasn't expressed. Her body isn't resisting and her breath is even, so I don't think I'm going too hard.

"Yep. It's fine," she replied in an unusually flat tone.

I wonder what she's not telling me. I can tell something is wrong. Maybe I did or said something wrong when I greeted her? Maybe she's not up for touch today and she's only here out of a sense of obligation because she made an appointment? I mentally scanned through our conversation and the previous two sessions for a clue. Having worked with many clients who have a touch-trauma history, and knowing that sometimes bodywork can bring up those memories or emotions, I was feeling concern for her—wanting to make sure she was completely at ease and feeling safe—while at the same time feeling a hint of frustration from the lack of communication inside.

"Would you like a little deeper or softer? How's the temperature? Is everything comfortable?" I gently prodded, hoping for a little clarification on how I could make it better for her.

I don't want to be doing anything wrong or making her uncomfortable.

"Nope. It's good," she replied, her words contradicting everything I was observing.

Well, sometimes people just aren't as into it. You have no idea what else is going on in her life right now. Leave her be and keep listening to her body and follow its guidance. If she is not ready to share, it is no place of yours to force it, the voice of wisdom and years of training and experience gently reminded me.

When the session was complete, I told her to take her time getting up and I would meet her downstairs. As I stepped out of the room, I felt something nagging in my stomach.

You did all you could at the moment. I'm sure everything is fine.

Yes, but you can feel the disconnection, my massage brain said. *And that's not how it was her first two sessions.* I walked down the stairs, through the busy salon, saying hello to a couple of the stylists, and grabbed her a glass of water. The discomfort was still sitting in my stomach as I made my way back to the front desk in time for her arrival.

"Here's your water." I handed it to her over the counter as I stood behind the computer. "How is everything feeling now that you've had an opportunity to move a bit in gravity?"

"Good," she said, handing me her credit card. She pulled out her phone. "Do you have anything next week?"

Okay, I must just be sensitive today. If she wasn't satisfied or I did something inappropriate for her needs, she wouldn't be making another appointment.

We finished the transaction and I walked around the counter—my now-preferred way of opening the possibility of a tap on the shoulder, handshake, or hug goodbye.

"Have a lovely day and I'll see you next week. As you know, drink a lot of water," I reminded her, getting ready for the touch on the arm she usually gave me (and I returned) when she left.

"Yep." She turned abruptly, avoiding my eyes or any contact as she walked swiftly toward the door.

Aww. I hope she's able to work through whatever's bothering her today, I thought, a little twinge of empathy hitting my heart, while at the same time noticing my failure to keep my concern about my developing practice away from her experience on the table. *You were trying to make sure she was safe and comfortable for her, not just for your practice. This is one of your patterns—wanting to nurture everyone so they feel emotionally stable and calm when they leave. Sometimes people make a different choice, and that's their right.*

Losing Sight of the Destination and Wandering Aimlessly

Yes, sometimes people make different choices, and that's their right, I repeated to myself as the memory faded. *I really wanted a connected hug with my dad but he made a different choice, even if it was buried in unconscious routine. But why didn't I communicate my needs?*

I turned onto one of the main streets, quickly sorting through all of the possibilities for my silence.

I guess it's like many relationships. Once we get into a certain pattern, we just roll with it, no matter how we feel about it. I thought back to other hugs I shared with my parents. *Yep, at some point in time, hugs became a habitual, rote acknowledgment of what we express through words, instead of communicating our feelings through intentional touch.*

But I knew it went far beyond hugs, and far beyond myself.

A lot of people talk about how they aren't feeling loved by the touch they receive in their relationships. It's either lacking, overwhelming, or not the right sort. Yet no one seems to have honest discussions about what they need. It ends up being a giving and a tolerating, instead of both people really enjoying it.

I thought about my friend Michelle, who is certified as a professional cuddler, and how surprised I was when she mentioned how many men in relationships have hired her because they felt like they wanted the ability to snuggle without any pressure or expectation to perform with their partners.

> **Did You Know?**
>
> Professional Cuddlers (a.k.a. cuddlists) are certified professionals you can hire to snuggle with you platonically. We are so deprived of touch today that this service is offered widely across the U.S. and Europe. While everyone remains fully clothed during the G-rated sessions, cuddling provides individuals a safe space to feel respected, accepted, and worthy for exactly who they are—while also getting a natural dose of oxytocin, serotonin, and dopamine.

I guess no matter how safe the environment is, or how well we know someone, there is still an opportunity to figure out how to develop more safety for ourselves and those with whom we want to share physical connection.

I took a long deep breath, exhaling out some of the anxiety and frustration.

This situation with my dad should be easier than most. I know he loves me and would want me to feel safe enough to speak up and ask for what I want. Plus, I know he would enjoy it as well.

Sitting at a stoplight, I let my mind drift back to a time where I wished I had the strength to trust my body's sense of safety and speak my truth.

An Unforeseen Storm

I walked up to the rambler-style house in the residential neighborhood and knocked on the door. "Welcome." The slightly taller, slightly bald, casually-dressed sixty-year-old man I'd met at the health fair the week before greeted me, stepping back from the door and sweeping his arm back in a gesture to enter. "Come on in. You can leave your shoes on. We're going to head this way." He pointed through a wide, open doorway into a living room where an older woman was seated on a couch, feet propped up on the coffee table in front of her.

"This is my wife, Evelyn," he said from behind me as I entered the living room and he closed the door.

"Hello." I greeted her as I walked over to shake her hand, "I'm Dawn."

"Hi," she smiled tiredly as she gave a cold, semi-limp handshake. "Sorry I'm not getting up. My body just doesn't move the way it used to, especially in cold like this."

I nodded. *I wonder if he gives her massages, or if she's like my dad who avoids them unless the pain is really overwhelming or I'm really convincing.*

"We're going to head downstairs. That's where I've got my room set up. Just follow me," he said, walking through the living room to the stairs that led into the dark basement. The room was pleasantly warm, and I took in the space, with its old-style wood paneling walls and tiny window in the upper far corner.

Reminds me of my parent's basement, I noted. *But it's warm and the massage table looks cozy.* The table in the center had light-colored sheets and what looked like a soft, thick blanket on top. There was a chair in the corner near the window, and I walked over to it, assuming it was set up for me.

"Is there anything in particular you are looking for today?" Ed inquired, as I turned to face him.

I thought about our brief interaction at the health fair. He had given me a great five-minute chair massage, and when he found out I was a massage therapist as well, he'd asked me to critique a new routine.

"Nope. I know you want to practice some things. I'll let you know if I don't like it. I tend to prefer deep pressure, but do whatever you're comfortable with. Don't feel you have to hurt yourself to impress me," I guided, knowing that an intentional pressure of any kind felt better than a forced deep massage, especially when it wasn't skillful.

"Great. You know the routine, so I guess I don't have to tell you anything. Just go ahead and get undressed, leave your clothes on the chair, and start facedown." He left the room and closed the door gently behind him.

I undressed quickly, hopped on the table, and made myself comfortable. *I'm so ready for this,* I sighed. *I really need to get back into a regular routine of massage self-care.*

My body accustomed to the cues, I started drifting off into a deep relaxed state. A knock on the door brought me out of my reverie.

"Come in," I projected, head down in the face cradle.

He came into the room and asked, "Are you comfortable?" as he laid his hands on my back over the blanket and got ready to begin the massage.

"Yep," I replied, nodding even though my head was in a hole.

After he had uncovered my back and massaged for about ten minutes, Ed's voice broke into my trance. "If you are enjoying what I'm doing, just feel free to moan, so I know I'm doing okay."

What? My eyes shot open in surprise, and I saw the thick patterned carpet under me. *Oh yeah, I'm supposed to be giving him feedback,* I thought, a bit shocked by his word choice, but guilty I hadn't been following through on my part of the bargain.

That's weird, my inner voice confirmed. *You should have him clarify his words.*

I'm sure he's just nervous, my rational part argued. *Stop overreacting.*

"It's been good. Your pressure has been consistent, and you are using a nice variety of strokes."

"Great. Well, just feel free to make noise if you like it. Then you don't have to say anything."

Okay. That's creepy. I vowed not to make any noise, but didn't correct his word choice again. *He's just old. It's probably a generation-gap miscommunication.* But my red flags were up, and I was a bit on edge.

He finished my back, covered it again, and moved to my right leg. He undraped it appropriately, applied the oil, and started working.

"Does that feel good?" he asked.

My discomfort grew again, but my people-pleasing nature rolled with the flow. "Yes," I replied simply.

"I'm going to do a stretch for your quad," he said as he pulled my leg high in the air. I felt and knew I was completely exposed.

In shock and disbelief, I pushed my leg back down to the table. "I don't like that," I said firmly, even as I felt myself going a bit numb and disconnecting from my body. "That's really not a good way to stretch someone."

What is going on here? Is this how he's been taught? Can't he understand or feel how I am perceiving this? My mind raced for logical answers as I ignored my instincts. I lay there, continuing to let him touch me as my mind raced. *Anything I say now to stop him and end the session is going to sound like an accusation. I should have said something earlier.* Social training and self-blame took over as I justified all the reasons why I wasn't speaking up for myself and tolerating the situation in the moment. No longer relaxed in any manner, I waited anxiously for the hour to be over.

"Okay, that concludes the session," he said, brushing down my legs through the sheets. "Just come out when you are done and meet me in the living room."

When he closed the door behind him, I hurriedly jumped off the table and ran to the security of my clothes. Hunched over and covering myself, as if he was watching me get dressed from behind, I turned around and gave my middle finger to the doorway he had just exited.

Seriously, Dawn? You are flicking off an empty room? Nice overreaction, Drama Queen. Just get dressed and get out of here.

I walked back up to the living room, where Ed was chatting with his wife and his next client, who was also in her sixties.

"Dawn, meet Shirley," Ed said as he gestured to the new arrival. She's from my church and has also been letting me practice on her.

See, you were totally overreacting. His wife wouldn't be sitting there all happy with a repeat client if this had actually been going on. Yes, you could have been clearer on what he was doing wrong, but his intention was not to be sexual.

Despite my twisted logic, I felt like I needed a shower when I got home.

Recovering From a Setback Rebuilding Camp

Through the construction zone finally, I shook my head, as if I could shake out those images and all the body memories that came with them. *I really wish I'd said something. Of course, now I know for sure that he deserved a good correction.* The last part of that story flickered in fast snapshots across my mind. A phone call from the police department. Questions about my profession and whether it was common to touch in certain places and with particular tools, and whether I had received a massage from him and how it went. The realization that he had been sexually assaulting women. The feeling of my experience being justified. The regret of not correcting or reporting him.

You did the best you could in the moment. Not confronting him was also a way to keep yourself safe. You were in a vulnerable position, and even though you could have kicked his ass if he had pushed something, that's not really the way you roll.

I let my mind drift off into an imaginary scenario where I spoke up, kicked his butt, and prevented all of the other women from having their sense of safety taken from them, before I brought it back to the matter at hand.

I know I will regret it if I say nothing to my dad, not because of anything he's done, but because it's something I want and need and—I paused, thinking about the fact that I was leaving again for six months and when I returned they would be in Florida for the winter. *I am going to change how I hug them from now on,* I resolved. *Who knows how much time I have left with them.* The thought sobered me as I brought my attention back to the road.

It's time to experiment with ways to re-engage touch with my dad and my family. It shouldn't be that hard, since they are already accustomed to touch. I just need to be more intentional about it.

As I turned left onto the street where my wellness center was, I remembered the surprising opportunity to re-engage touch in a community that valued physical connection.

Playful Interactions on the Trail

I walked into the busy, modern-styled, open-air, farm-to-table restaurant and headed toward the open staircase near the back. The sound of small groups conversing over dinner gave way to the excited chatter of women's voices as I arrived at the top of the stairs and turned toward the conference dining room. I admired the view of the river through the large windows and stepped through the door.

"Hey Dawn, welcome back!" Victoria, the leader of the business connection group greeted me. "Make sure you sign in there on the table and leave your business cards so people who want to connect with you can grab them." She smiled and opened her arms, and another professionally-dressed woman swooped in from behind me and exuberantly greeted her with a full-force hug.

Wow, this is so different than any business group I have even been to before. I scanned the room to see a variety of well-dressed women greeting each other with hugs and touches to each other's arms. *The first time I was here, I thought it was an anomaly; but it really is the culture of the group. After the "shaming incident", I had forgotten that people could even hug at business events unless they were long-time friends.*

Or sometimes not even then, my inner voice reminded me as I turned to the table to sign in.

Enough, I hushed it. *This seems like a safe place where touch is allowed.* I pulled out my business cards and set them on the table, scanning the cards already there to remind myself of any names of the women I had forgotten since the previous meeting. I stepped away from the registration table and headed toward the U-shaped tables where places were set with water and the evening's agenda. I plopped my stuff down in a chair next to one with a bright red purse, and opened myself to meeting some new people.

I feel really at-home in this group, even though I barely know anyone. I turned to walk over to the nearest threesome, feeling confidence and the warmth in my chest as I strode toward them. *In most other business meetings, I still feel a bit hesitant joining a group unless I'm invited in, but here it feels like everyone is so warm and welcoming.*

"...day job is boring, so I joined this group as a writer and so I could meet more fun people," one woman finished. From behind, she looked like a tall, dark-haired Viking; and I remembered her from the previous two meetings.

"Yeah," the shorter, curly-haired blonde chimed in, "I can't wait to transition from my day job into my home business. I'm really close to that goal." Her eyes met mine and she paused to welcome me in. "Hi, I'm Jessica!" She smiled and reached out her hand. "Welcome. Is this your first meeting?"

"My third," I replied, shaking her hand and then smiling at the group. "I'm Dawn. Nice to see you again!" I nodded to the Viking as I searched my brain for her name. "How's the book coming?"

"Oh, I'm back to doing more research," she replied. "I'm writing a different book at the moment as well, which I hope to have out this fall. It's much more causal and is just my observations on people and life."

"I can't wait to read it!" Jessica said enthusiastically, briefly touching the Viking on her arm to emphasize her point.

Freya. Her name is Freya. She lives in the cities, about forty-five minutes from here.

"I'm Gina," the woman to my left said, eyes sparkling as she leaned in and deliberately laid her hand briefly and warmly on my arm. "I'm a commercial realtor from the area."

"Good evening, everybody! It's such a great night to be here, and what a beautiful view of the river." A bouncy, energetic thirty-something glided into the circle, hugging Jessica as she spoke and then turned toward Gina. "Hey, I'm Jennifer. I saw you at the other chapter meeting, but didn't get to actually meet you. I'm a hugger. Do you want a hug?"

I smiled at Jennifer's ease. *This must be a really safe place if that's how she's introducing herself. I wonder if she'll introduce herself to me in the same way?*

"Okay everybody, take your seats and let's get started," Victoria prompted loudly over the chatter.

"Hi," Jennifer said quickly, placing her hand on my arm as the circle broke and we moved toward our seats.

Yep, she totally would have hugged me if we hadn't been interrupted, I thought. *I used to be like that. Maybe she and I can connect when the meeting is done.*

I sat in my seat and introduced myself to the red-purse woman quietly and tuned into Victoria's introduction, already in progress. "...We are a connection company. We believe when we make strong connections first, business naturally follows."

I'm already learning a lot from these women. I feel so open and myself here—like I used to at business events. I don't feel like I'm pretending or trying to position myself as a business owner rather than "just a massage therapist," like I have been lately. It feels more ethical and real to just be who I am. All I need to do is to authentically connect to be part of this community.

Embracing the Next Stage

Turning into the parking lot of my new wellness center, I found a parking spot quickly and hopped out with my things.

That's what I want—to be who I am and to authentically connect with my parents and others while I'm with them.

Determined and motivated to be intentional about asking for what I want and need, I walked in to start my day with clients.

Remedies
Evaluating Safety on
The Route Moment by Moment

"Safety" is a big buzz word these days, especially when it comes to touch. Unfortunately, the conversations are usually focused on developing external spaces or controls for safety rather than tuning in with our own individual sense of safety on an ongoing basis.

So, here is our chance.

I have realized over the years that safety is experienced on a spectrum, rather than just existing or not. We experience it in physical, mental, and emotional spheres; and we often use our conditioning, observations, and gut feelings to determine where on the spectrum we are—from life-threatening danger to complete safety.

The point is, safety is not static. It is subject to change based on a multitude of factors.

For example, speaking our insecurities to a friend may feel completely safe at one moment, and completely overwhelming and unsafe another. One day it might feel completely safe to talk about our financial frustration, and the next it may make us feel vulnerable or judged. Our physical safety can feel different in the same spaces day-to-day depending on environment, energy levels, emotional state, and the energy of others around us.

The same concept applies as we discuss safety with regard to touch. What may feel easy and safe one day may not the next. For example, giving a hug to your partner after a lovely meal and conversation can feel much safer, intentional, and connected than one given after an argument before it is fully resolved. This contrast in safety is okay. In fact, it is a great opportunity to reflect and begin to understand your physical and mental signals at a deeper level. Is there something you are picking up subconsciously? What is different now than before? By heightening our awareness we can become clearer around what we really want in this situation/experience and try to put words to it.

In seventh grade I had a good friend, whose father was a martial arts instructor, who invited me to join her every week at the gym to learn the art of self-defense. I loved it and continued practicing until I went to massage school. Because of that training I always had a strong sense of physical safety. When I was out with friends I felt I could protect myself and them if needed. If I was feeling emotionally vulnerable, I would adopt a bad-ass attitude to create a sense of safety around me.

This also allowed me to use more physical contact in my life. Because I did not have to worry about physical safety, I felt free to express my desire for connection with others through physical touch on the arm, shoulder, back, hugs—whatever I wanted that felt appropriate to me and the situation at the time.

Several decades of life and massage experience have taught me that not everyone is so lucky.

Some of us have been taught we do not get to decide what happens to our bodies. We have learned to ignore our internal "red flags," or that our wishes are not as important as the wishes of others. Some of us give or tolerate because it is easier than saying *no*. Sometimes we just don't know what we want and do not have the tools, skills, or time to delve into it. And sometimes the safety message we get from others through body language or tone-of-voice signals are incongruous with our own sense of safety, desire, or intuition, and we get confused within ourselves.

Why does this happen? Well, we have nerve cells in our brain called mirror neurons. On a simplistic level, these neurons help us relate the "what" an action is (like a smile or a touch) to the "why"—the intention—of the action. Mirror neurons are attributed to things like people smiling back when you smile at them, or adapting the same posture as you if they feel connected while moving away from similar postures if there is an emotional dislike or distrust. Our brains are constantly evaluating risk. The safer we feel the more our bodies and brains can let go of fight/flight/freeze states and move into a place of a calm body, prosocial behavior, and trust—which includes a lot of mirroring of those states and behaviors.[36]

However, in extreme cases, safety (physical, emotional, or situational) can feel threatening to some people's nervous systems. Our reptilian brain (which controls our body's vital functions such as heart rate and breathing) and our limbic brain (which is partially responsible for emotions) are responsible for our fight, flight, freeze responses and do their best to evaluate and react to situations to keep us safe. People who grew up in or had a lot of experience in unsafe situations register safety as unsafe because they've never experienced it before. It's an unknown.

With this in mind, finding a route to safety and having resources to support us is key. Even those of us with strong tools and body awareness can make mistakes and have moments where we allow our boundaries—large or small—to be crossed or violated, as you saw in my story with the icky wanna-be therapist. However, with help and self-forgiveness, we can move past mistakes and continue to grow and connect with those around us.

The point is, healthy, appropriate touch requires us to be connected with our bodies and our emotions; and to stop believing that sex is always part of the conversation when touch is a topic.

Touch is the most basic and primitive form of communication, and is intrinsically (by its nature) emotional. There is no sensation without emotion. Our sense of touch is created by many sensors working in parallel. When we are touched, the nerve signals are processed by two systems in the brain. The first is the somatosensory cortex which processes facts including: where am

I being touched, in what manner, and how intensely? The second is the insula, which is part of our emotional touch system. In other words, our brain interprets our sensory experience into emotion.

When we start to recognize what styles of touch are linked to particular emotions and/or sensations in our own body it brings clarity. When someone touches you gently you may interpret it as more compassionate than if they had used firm contact, or you may interpret it as more sexual. Being conscious of our touch roots brings with it an ability to discern true safety—not just what our brains have been conditioned to perceive as safe.

For example, when I am at a friend's house and meet someone new and they hug me, I presume they are doing it out of the comfort of being in a safe place, and I can make the decision at that moment regarding how I want to react. I can accept, educate, or say *no*. I know that when Lance hugs me there is no sexual energy to it no matter how long or short the hug. I know that when a friend suddenly grabs me on my arm, my first instinct is that the need for my attention is urgent because I surround myself with people who make me feel safe. However, if a stranger in a crowd grabs me on my arm hard suddenly, my martial arts background kicks in and my instinct is to disconnect the contact and prepare for attack. Yet because I'm aware there is a potential that someone has tripped and grabbed me to steady themselves I allow time for my brain to process before doing anything rash. If I am in a crowd and someone brushes my low back, I am going to give the generous assumption that it was an accident unless their body language says otherwise. Understanding your own reaction and the source of the emotion that is triggered may prevent misperception around physical contact.

My favorite example of this is the warm/cold coffee experiment. In a study done at Yale University by John Bargh, forty-one undergraduates were asked to hold a cup of either warm or cold coffee while in an elevator where they were told they were going to be assisting in a different experiment. The undergraduates completed a questionnaire, in which there was a description of an individual. The people who had held the warm coffee were more likely to associate that individual with warm traits (generous, happy, good-natured) versus cold traits (ungenerous, unhappy, irritable, etc.)[37]

As I searched further, I found Bargh's reply to an article stating the study was not able to be replicated. He states, "several brain imaging studies—much of it from the Naomi Eisenberger lab at UCLA—directly supported our hypothesis of an actual anatomical link in human insula between the region reactive to physical warmth and a nearby region reactive to social warmth. In their several studies, either type of warmth activated both regions. When participants held something warm, or when they texted family and friends, the same insular region became active."[38]

Touch also can create a sense of safety that can become stronger as we are more connected to another. Sixteen married women were put into an fMRI machine, and their brains were studied while they were under threat of electric shock. They were evaluated in three different ways—while holding their husband's hand, a male stranger's hand, and no hand at all. The brain responded less to the threat of shock holding a stranger's hand than no hand at all, and even less when holding their husband's hand. The stronger the marital relationship was reported to be, the less threat was detected. In an amusing 2013 Tedx Talk, Dr. James Coan, one of the researchers in the above study, mentioned that when they look at what the brain is doing when the shock is directed to a friend or romantic partner, the stress patterns in the brain look similar to the pattern in self. When the shock was directed at a stranger, the brain patterns looked different.[39]

Another study was done in which a barrier was placed between two unacquainted people. One person was instructed to attempt to communicate emotion through a one-second touch to the other, based upon a set list of emotions.[40] According to an article by Dacher Keltner, who was one of the researchers in this study, "the odds of guessing the right emotion by chance were about eight percent... participants guessed compassion correctly nearly sixty percent of the time. Gratitude, anger, love, fear—they got those right more than fifty percent of the time as well."[41]

These research studies help us understand not only how the brain links the sense of touch with emotion, but also how developing warm relationships that include touch can enhance feelings of safety and connection.

Did You Know?

"Touching is a sign of familiarity, friendship, and respect. When we touch someone in passing, it can increase the likelihood that they will **respond to us with greater positive regard** and the desire to help."[42]

The nation's 75 million millennials (born between 1981 and 1996) and Generation Z adults (born between 1997 and 2012) are lonelier than any other U.S. demographic and report being in worse health than older generations. In addition, 54% of respondents said they feel no one knows them well, and four in 10 reported they "lack companionship," their "relationships aren't meaningful" and they "are isolated from others."[43]

Increasing warm touch among couples has a beneficial influence on multiple stress-sensitive systems.[44]

"Research out of Carnegie Mellon indicates that feeling connected to others, especially through physical touch, protects us from stress-induced sickness. Hugs give stress-buffering social support. The more often people hugged, the less likely they were to get sick."[45]

> When you initiate physical contact you may reap all the same benefits as those you touch. For example, Tiffany Field's research has revealed that a person giving a massage experiences as great a reduction in stress hormones as the person on the receiving end.[46]

An Internal Peek

How do you nurture yourself when you want more touch or feel overwhelmed by touch?

For some playful ways to incorporate safe touch in your own life on your own, I invite you to turn to the "Play and Explore" section for chapter two in the back of this book.

"If it is important to you, you will find a way. If not, you'll find an excuse."

~ Ryan Blair, American entrepreneur and author ~

CHAPTER 3
CROSSROADS & CHOICES
Tackling the Mountain of Wants, Needs, and Consent

Looking Up from the Base of the Mountain

Mmmmm. The smell of freshly brewed coffee made me smile the minute I walked into the cozy coffee shop. Pausing to let my eyes adjust to the dimmer lighting, I took the moment to look around. Big comfortable couches and coffee tables, large soft chairs that are broken in just right, and regular tables of all sizes were placed intentionally throughout the space, making it a favorite spot for individuals working on their computers or for families and small groups to connect.

Kinda busy today, I thought as I searched for an empty spot. I eyed up a small table in the corner where I could work while still being able to see outside as well as "people watch." *You would get a lot more done if you didn't set yourself up to watch everyone. But then, why would you be here if you didn't want to be sidetracked a bit today?* I dropped off my water bottle and laptop, grabbed my wallet, walked to the counter, and ordered my white-chocolate Americano from the friendly baristas. As I was waiting for my drink, I studied the art on the walls. They had a great energy and added to the atmosphere—calm enough to not draw attention but colorful enough to give the place a sense of vibrancy and aliveness. Every time I looked at them I saw something a little different.

You've got two hours to get those emails done, do some marketing for EFT, and get all of your certifications renewed before you head out of town. Plus, the few assignments for your class and mentorship. You should write a business newsletter and blog, since you haven't done one since you've returned, as well as figure out what else you need to purchase before leaving for Europe again. So, stay away from social media, I coached myself as I walked back to my table with my coffee, determined to write in an espresso-fueled frenzy and get everything done.

Emotional Freedom Techniques

"EFT Tapping (a.k.a. tapping or EFT) helps us tune in to the negative patterns that we form around our uncomfortable thoughts, feelings, or troubling memories. We 'tap' on the correct pressure points while bringing the thoughts or emotions into consciousness."[47] The aim of EFT is to establish calm, conquer challenging emotions, and facilitate healing for emotional or physical issues.

I started my emails with intention, but it wasn't long before my attention drifted to the table off to my right. A toddling boy, perhaps three years old with sand-colored hair and a blue-striped shirt, had wandered away from the low, wooden coffee table piled with a variety of papers with colorful scribbles and crayons. He had a colorful masterpiece in hand, and was trying to climb up into his mother's lap. "Mom, Mom, Mommy, lookit. Mommy lookit." His voice grew louder with every word. She was sitting in an armchair, her back to me, cell phone trapped between left ear and shoulder, trying to write something down on the piece of paper she held on her right knee. She kept nudging him back with her left elbow and arm, trying to capture whatever was being said to her on the phone. When he continued to insist on her attention, she peeked up at him and shushed him a bit, glanced at the paper, and pointed back to the forgotten artwork on the table.

Awww, he's so cute. And so excited about his artwork. I smiled to myself as he continued to wave it before dropping it on the floor and attempting to climb onto her lap. *It's so hard when we have different needs at the moment. He wants attention, and she wants a few minutes of peace so she can finish this conversation. I wonder what the easiest compromise would be? How could she validate him and give him what he needs, while also still taking care of her needs?* Realizing she wasn't going to win this time around, she rearranged her phone to her right, scooped him up into her left lap, and tried to continue taking notes. He settled immediately, snuggled into her shoulder, and watched me with big eyes. *He's adorable,* I thought, smiling and waggling my fingers at him, as he smiled shyly and tucked his head down for a moment.

Kids are so clear about what they want and need, especially around touch, and the parents have to decide what they can accommodate in that moment. Almost like consent—do they want the touch as well, or are they allowing touch for the child, or are they allowing touch for themselves because it keeps the child quiet, or are they going to practice saying no? I pondered this interesting thought for a bit. *I wonder if the mom is aware of her own feelings around the touch, or if she is focused only on the interruption.* He peeked his head up playfully from the safety of his mother's lap. I ducked behind my computer screen a bit, and slowly picked my head up, eyes on his. He giggled and ducked again.

It's hard to accommodate the demands of children when they conflict with our time schedules and obligations in the moment. Or maybe she, just like my dad, is not the touchy-feely kind of parent. I hope he has at least one affectionate person in his life. My mom has always been that safe place for me.

The Easier Trail Goes Around the Mountain

"So, are you coming to visit me in Sweden while I'm traveling? Or are you going to wait and see if I actually get a job and work permit while I'm there?" I asked my mom one morning as we sat at the kitchen table in the sunshine. I was finalizing my plans for my first trip alone to Europe.

"I'm going to wait for now and see where you land," she replied, smiling back at me as she set down her steaming cup of coffee. "If I book tickets and then you have to leave Sweden, or you end up in a different area, it could get quite complicated. Besides, it's my last year at work before I retire, and I should probably finish it out before I travel for any length of time."

"Except Florida though, right?" I replied playfully.

"Well, yes. At least there I'm on a similar time zone and can mail my work back and forth if needed," she justified. "Besides, I haven't been feeling quite right lately. I don't know what's going on, but the last few months, my body has just been tired and achy and not well."

Wow. She usually doesn't complain like that. Usually it's about her hip, but now that she's had the replacement, she's been pretty good. A few months of symptoms sounds serious.

"Okay! That allows me more flexibility anyway," I answered cheerfully, hiding my concern for her health and focusing on my intention that we would be able to enjoy travel together again.

It was really fun when we visited Sweden last year. We got into such a rhythm. Lots of hugs and cuddling on the couch while deciding the plan for the day. We shared a lot with each other in those six weeks, especially since we didn't have cell phones to distract us on a regular basis. I hope when I get my permit, she'll come over and will be able to be as active as before.

The sudden pit in my stomach surprised me.

I've only been here a week, and I'm already feeling the loss of what I had the first day with them—lots of time to talk, long and comforting hugs, and a few shared meals. It's amazing how fast we defaulted to the pattern of quick hugs and the casual, comfortable routines that come with living together.

"Well, I should get my run in before I go to work. I'm going to make a smoothie when I get back. Do you want some?" I stood up and slammed the rest of my coffee, against my better judgment.

"I already have one prepped in the fridge for myself. I'll throw some extra in it, and it will be ready when you get back," she replied, standing up as well. "Then I need to get down and get my report ready for the board meeting this week."

"YAY! Thanks, Mom." I walked over and gave her a long, appreciative hug.

I really need to make an effort to keep these up. I know hugging is really important to her. I shouldn't let it become something automatic and insignificant.

On my run I thought about the pit in my stomach and my relationship with my mom. After that first trip together, we had committed to keep up our strong level of communication and spend a lot of time together.

I didn't follow through on that part of the bargain at all. I let my work and general busyness get in the way like usual. She even asked to schedule a night out with me and my sister, and I told her I didn't have time before leaving. That wasn't very daughterly of me. I didn't even make time for drive-by hugs on my way through the area. Well, too late to fix that now that you live with them.

I thought about all the people that were scrambling to get into my schedule one more time before I left. *I better just get a few dates for Mom, Dad, and me to hang out before I leave. We should do something that really intentionally connects us, like dancing. We always seem to have more fun dancing to a good band. And there are always lots of hugs on the dance floor when the songs are done.*

A few nights later, I decided to make it happen.

Walking into the living room where they were watching the evening television lineup, I started, "We should find a time for us to all hang out before I go. I've only got a few nights left open in the next three weeks before I fly out."

"Are you still coming to the cabin with us next weekend?" My dad asked, referring to my sister and nephews as well.

"Yes, but I was wondering if there was another night. How about next Tuesday? Maybe we can find a place to go dancing?"

"It's hard to find places with bands unless it's a weekend," my dad replied, "or they start at my *bedtime*." His emphasis on the word made him chuckle. "I'm just not as young as I used to be. I can't go partying with you all night until 2 a.m. in the morning. Tuesday is also cribbage night with Cousin Rob."

"Oh yeah. Mondays and Thursdays I work late. How about a Wednesday?" I asked, hoping for at least dinner at home and time without television.

"Wednesdays are golf league and dinner with the golf girls," my mom said.

I forgot they are as busy as I am. Suddenly, the need to connect became even stronger. *Funny how easy it seems to connect when there is all the time in the world. But what if this is my last opportunity to connect with them before I go? I better make the best of that weekend at the cabin, even while keeping the boys entertained.*

I noticed that I felt let down and separated from them, and eyed up the space between them on the large couch. They each had their corner, and the middle cushion was open as usual. *It would be nice to just sneak in between the two of them on the couch. Make some time for some physical contact and connection right here, right now since the next few weeks don't look promising. But I better go start my massage laundry and unpack my dirty lunch containers first.*

"Okay, sounds like the cabin is going to be it," I said, part of me still longing to grab that space on the couch. "We will make that work." I walked out through the kitchen and down the stairs to put my first load of sheets in the washer. *May as well brush my teeth and stuff, too, since I'm down here near the guest bathroom.* I folded what was in the dryer, moved the clothes from the washer to the dryer, and was just putting in my massage sheets when I heard my mom yelling from the top of the stairs.

"Good night, Dawn. We are heading to bed! See you in the morning."

"Okay," I yelled back, "I'll be right up."

So much for hanging out with them tonight. I didn't think they were heading to bed this early, I thought as I glanced at my watch. *Oh, already 10:30 p.m. That happened fast. I guess the news was on when I was up there. I just wasn't paying attention.* I shoved everything in the washer and hustled upstairs, but my parents were already in their room, door shut for the night. *Man, not even a goodnight hug. They couldn't wait a few minutes?* I turned and trudged to the kitchen, cleaned up my dishes, and then finished getting ready for bed. *Tomorrow, I will make sure to ask them to give me hugs before they sneak off to bed. It makes me feel really unimportant when it seems they don't even want to wait a couple minutes for me.*

Caught in my own story, I didn't even consider they were in the midst of their habitual routines; and I could have checked in before heading downstairs to see how much longer they were going to be up.

I guess I should have snuck on the couch when I had a chance. Feeling decidedly pouty, I finished getting ready for bed and snuggled under the covers, feeling sorry for myself and decidedly alone.

Moving Forward With Confidence

Ugh, it sucks to want a hug from a parent and have to demand one. I feel ya, kiddo! I thought as I took another sip of my Americano and smiled at the boy. He had climbed off his mom's lap and was fully engaged with coloring again.

His touch bucket must be full again. I wish mine was!

I was looking at the pictures from my first trip to Europe on the screen in front of me, wondering which I should include in my blog, when a peal of laughter made me look up again. A group of three fifty-something women had walked to a four-top table near me and sat down. Of course, I couldn't help but eavesdrop.

"Overall it was a good date though, and the waiter apologized profusely for dropping our dinners on him," one woman said, flopping down in the chair with her back to the boy and his mom. She set her large tan purse on the ground and tucked her dark, cropped hair back behind her ear in one smooth motion.

"It sounds like he took it well though," her tall blonde friend said. Bracelets jangling and diamond rings flashing, she set her white handbag carefully on the table and took the seat opposite. "Better than your ex would have reacted, for sure."

"A cute single guy with an easygoing sense of humor is nothing to scoff at, at our age," said another dark-haired woman, dressed business casual, as she slid smoothly into her seat facing me. "From what you said, it also sounds like he doesn't have too much baggage with his ex, and his daughter is out of the house. So, win-win there." She smiled suggestively and winked at the storyteller.

"Oh, that reminds me. After the game and before the restaurant, we ended up going to this little local distillery to have a drink. It was pretty busy, so I sat and he stood while we had our drinks. Can I show you what he did?" The storyteller leaped out of her chair and stood behind the businesswoman, one hand on her shoulder.

"Since this is public, I am assuming this is a G-rated demo?" The seated women broke into another round of laughter. "I'm up for whatever. You know I love touch, too."

"You know how much I always complained that Tom didn't touch me unless he wanted sex," the storyteller rushed on. "But this guy just kept his hand kind of protectively on my shoulder, just like this while we were ordering and waiting for drinks. And then kept doing this really nice gentle-but-firm thing on my neck," she said, as she moved her palm up the opposite side of her friend's neck and back down with her thumb.

"Oh my goodness, that tickles!" The businesswoman squirmed and pushed her hand off. "Stop it!"

The storyteller looked surprised. "Really? I loved it! Maybe I'm not doing it right or my nails are just too long, but it was so soothing. He checked in to make sure it felt okay to me, and it was so nice just to have touch without being sexual..." She dropped her voice and said something as she sat back down that made all three of them giggle again.

"But seriously," she said, bringing her voice up again as she playfully swatted the blonde's arm from across the table, "it was so nice to have a guy touch with respect and attention, while also checking in to make sure it was okay."

I smiled to myself broadly and looked back at my screen, trying to focus on my work as they brought it down to lower tones again.

I love how many older women have such confidence in their touch boundaries.

I remembered one of my mom's friends in Florida telling me, "Honey, the older I get, the less I care about what others think of me. I'm just going to tell people like it is, and force them to treat me the way I deserve."

I think I'm finally hitting that age as well. I'm sure all of this touch training has helped so I don't have to wait until I'm seventy-something to set boundaries. My touch has become much better with my friends again, and I'm really learning to ask for what I need with them. I have come a long way from that "shaming incident;" and even though it sucks that I went through so much turmoil and guilt around it, it really has helped me become a lot more mindful around touch for myself and others.

I looked back at the pictures on my computer and started scanning through older pictures as well, suddenly nostalgic for some of the times I'd had with groups of my friends.

I need to reconnect with some of the more touch-comfortable groups I used to hang out with. I haven't done a very good job of that since I've been back. Wow, was it ten years ago already that I started camping with this group? I looked at a couple of pictures with me and some then-new friends around a campfire. *I sure learned a lot about touch from them as well.*

The Path Less Traveled

"I'm really struggling with this decision." My confession finally emerged, my eyes downcast at the grass, my head hung in shame. Even though Charlie, Laura, and I only met five years prior at this annual camping event, it felt like we were old friends. They listened patiently, sitting on fold-out chairs around the unlit fire pit, a few of the sun's rays peeking through the trees as it crept under the horizon. It felt both freeing and shaming to finally share that I had burned myself out and was in a deep place of confusion about whether or not to close my business and leave my employees jobless, essentially giving up all I had built over thirteen years. *I can't believe I'm sharing this on what's supposed to be a fun and happy camping weekend.* Although I only saw these people yearly, five years of hugs, laughter, and campfire stories had made me feel right at home.

"I almost didn't even come here this year." Tears started rolling down my face. *The idea of trying to act cheerful and give hugs felt so overwhelming. I don't want to bring anyone down, but I desperately need support, comfort, and touch.* "I also couldn't bear the thought of being alone all weekend. I'm sorry. We should change the subject."

"Hey, what do you need? How can I support you?" Charlie's question was so clear, so honest, and so open, I almost didn't know how to respond.

"I feel like I just want to be held and told it's all going to be okay."

"Great. Let's do it." His firm and gentle response stopped my tears as I snapped my head up and looked him in the eye. "It's probably more comfortable to cuddle in a tent. Would you prefer yours? Or mine?"

He can't be serious. Isn't that something only partners and parents do? My conditioned mind protested at the thought. *The offer sounds so peaceful and nurturing.* "Um, mine would be fine." The discomfort quickly passed as I remembered what a respectful and touch-communicative group I was in.

When a friend first brought me into this group, he had shared the basic rules of the game. Keep each other safe, respect each other's boundaries, have fun, and communicate your needs. *I have rarely witnessed any kind of touch that wasn't respectful here; and when someone does cross a line unintentionally, there are quick amends and behavioral adjustments.*

He stood up and offered me his arm. I took it and we headed to my tent. "As you know, if you decide you want me to leave at any time, just tell me."

I cannot believe all I had to do was ask for what I want, and it is so freely given. My heart was already opening, and my steps were already feeling lighter. *I know I've been burning the candle for many years, but I am sure the tipping point for my burnout is from lack of touch beyond getting massages.* I crawled in first, shoving my sleeping bag to the top of my sleeping pad to use as a pillow as I curled up on my side, dried tears still on my face. Charlie snuggled up behind me, acting as "big spoon."

"Where do you want my arm?" he asked, resting his hand gently on my hip.

I grabbed his arm and wrapped it around me, hanging onto his hand with both of mine and bringing it to the center of my chest. *Mmmm.* I sighed deeply as comfort washed over my body, feeling the gentle surge of oxytocin and serotonin as my mind calmed on its own for the first time in what seemed like months. *It's like an internal key has switched. I'm getting what I need, and it's all about me, just for this moment.* Tears started in my eyes again as a wave of gratitude and love washed over me.

"Hey Dawn," Charlie nudged me gently out of a sleep I hadn't realized I had fallen into. "How are you doing? I'm thinking of leaving you now, but you can keep sleeping."

"I'm really good, Charlie. Thank you so much." I replied sleepily. "It's so nice to be heard and cared for."

"Of course. You deserve to be cared for." He gave a light squeeze and kissed me quickly on the back of my head before climbing out of my tent. "As we all do."

He's so right. This group has taught me so much about respectful, compassionate, and consensual touch. I am really lucky I was introduced to them. With that thought, I drifted back off into a much-needed blissful sleep.

Perseverance in Adversity
Tenacity in the Ascent

Aagggh, just another amazing weekend with that group. I felt so connected to life and myself again when I left.

I took another sip of my Americano. *Enough old pictures. Get back to your blog,* I scolded myself, reorienting to the task at hand. I transitioned back to my Europe pictures, found a few I hadn't posted online anywhere yet, and downloaded them in a batch to my computer, then up to my blogging program. As I waited for the site to catch up with the sudden demand, I allowed my gaze to wander the room again. The mom and boy had gone, and the women were wrapping up their coffee chat, empty cups in front of them. *It's still busy, but looks like it's slowing down a bit,* I thought, glancing at my watch out of habit. *I suppose it's the natural flow of these places. There are still a lot of people on computers doing their work. I wonder if they are in transition for their day as well, or if many of them come here often just to work around people. It would be fun to come here often enough to connect with the regulars. I bet they have a great vibe if they want to do their work here.*

The front door opened, and a pair of teenagers walked through the door. He had a casual athletic look in jeans and a t-shirt, and was intently focused on the long-haired blonde who was completely engulfed in her phone as he held the door and guided her through with his hand on her low back. *Poor guy, I can see where this is going already. So many people seem to be immersed in their phones instead of the people they are with. It's really disconnecting all of us.* I had a moment of gratitude for my friends who are really good about leaving the phones down unless they are expecting a work communication. *But they always apologize that they will have to look at their phones and let me know why. It just seems like common courtesy.* I sighed, thinking of my waitstaff friends who complain about people spending longer at their tables because they are on their phones too much. *It cuts into social fabric financially and emotionally. It's really sad.* The phone-focused beauty flopped on the couch near where the boy had been playing earlier and looked up long enough to give him her order and put her feet up on the low coffee table.

From the way he's trying to communicate and touch her, it seems like they have a certain level of comfort, but she is not engaged at all. I started laying out my blog flow until I saw him sit down on the couch, a drink in each hand. She looked at him, smiled, grabbed the drink from his hand and, looking back at her phone, filled him in on whatever was going on. *He's listening to her. That's a good sign. Oh, but there, now she's completely in the phone again. Not even talking.* She set down her drink and went back to two-handed texting. I watched as he tried to say a few things to her, even touching her on her arm for a moment to try to get her attention as he chuckled and said something he thought was funny. Nothing worked. He received only short and distracted replies in response. *She'll look at him for a bit and say a few words, but obviously thinks whatever or whoever is on her phone takes precedence.* He set his drink on the table, slouched back into the couch with a resigned look on his face and pulled out his phone, letting his legs flop open so the left one rested against hers. *I wish I was closer,* I sighed with mixed emotions. *I used to always engage people at bars and coffee shops if they were open to talk.* I felt the urge to go pat him on the shoulder in a motherly way and let him know that it is okay, and maybe he should try to find a girl who isn't so absorbed in her own world. *Okay, Dawn, stop it. You probably did similar things as a teen, especially when you were shy and didn't know how to interact well. But the poor guy was just trying to give her attention, and she is completely oblivious. I guess we all have to learn how to communicate somewhere,* I thought, cringing as I remembered how one of my more recent friendships had suddenly gone so wrong.

Running Out of Steam...
Challenge Overtakes Excitement

"How about we go practice some martial arts in the park today?" My friend James asked, as he watched me shove a load of massage sheets into the wash machine at my house. "You mentioned you wanted to refresh your skills before heading overseas."

I closed the machine and threw a scoop of soap into the drawer. "Nah, I've already done about fifteen hours of massage in the last few days. I should probably let my hands rest."

Besides, I'm restless and would rather run than hang around and practice right now. I'd probably get annoyed and irritated and no one needs that. I really don't want to do anything for anyone else right now, including him.

"You sure? I've been playing with releases and tweaking the techniques to be easy on you and play to the strength you have in your kicks," he encouraged. "Plus, when we get back I can cook some dinner for us while you finish your laundry and client work."

"How about we go for a run? I should get some cardio in," I replied, moving past him to get to the kitchen and empty my lunchbox. *And I just think I'm too brain-dead to learn anything anyway.* "There's plenty of time to practice before I leave." *Maybe his knee is hurting him again. I should probably make sure he's okay before I force him to run.* "How is your body feeling today anyway? Are you in any pain?"

"Nah," he said, playfully puffing up, "I'm tough. I can handle any kind of run you throw my way."

I smiled and threw a semi-distracted smile over my shoulder as I cooed to my two cats who had heard me in the kitchen and were begging for their dinner. "Better get ready then, because I'm high-energy and had a ton of coffee today."

James and I had met while I was out with my friend, Evelyn, having sushi at the bar of a local restaurant. She and I often, whether together or alone, include strangers in conversations if they are open to engage; so when he sat down next to us, the three of us ended up having a great chat until his other friends showed up. Before I left, he asked to meet up again. I accepted and we went dancing three weeks later. While chatting on the phone in the intervening time, we clarified boundaries. Neither of us was looking to date, as he was recently out of a long marriage; and I was on my way out of the country for a year or so and did not want any complications. We were both open to forming friendships and making connections.

As our friendship grew, he was respectful with his physical contact. We had great communication around touch boundaries which gave us opportunities to be causal about it, touching each other for emphasis when we talked, plus tons of hugs and snuggles when we were watching movies. I could tell when he was in a lot of pain, which he often was, being an ex-racer and having had many crashes on cycles. If I started giving him little massages, he would tell me not to get into a healing role with him. He said that he was open to getting some massage here and there, but that he didn't want to become a project or for me to get into work mode. It was hard for me to find the line between offering healing touch and not stepping into healer mode. Sometimes, he would stop me and tell me not to give massage unless he could reciprocate; so, I taught him some massage techniques so he could work on my arms, shoulders, and neck. The intention was to create some reciprocity and balance.

I'm not even sure how it happened, but somewhere along the line I did shift into the healer/caretaker mode because it was so natural to me. And as our friendship changed, our level of communication did not keep up with what was needed in order to allow the whole relationship to shift with our changing needs, wants, and experiences. Eventually, we both stopped paying attention to how we were feeling about touch. I did not realize until much later that I had started feeling like I was over-giving. My brain would justify it with "I'm the one who asked if I could try that technique," or "I am the one who started working on his arm because I was bored with the movie; so since I had initiated it, it felt unfair to be upset and demand something different." Right? Nope. Not at all.

Suddenly, subtle layers of inequality had settled into my body and into my deeper consciousness. Because I didn't make a choice to tune into myself and see what was really truly going on, I started allowing other aspects of our friendship to exacerbate the feeling of inequality. Suddenly, his being twenty minutes late, even when communicated, became an issue and another bit of evidence that he did not value the friendship. Stuck in my own story of over-giving, I had no idea that he was feeling the same. He tried over and over to help me practice my martial arts before I went to Europe, and I kept putting it off. I knew I felt apathetic about it, but wasn't clear at the time why, even with his enthusiasm to help. As I kept putting it off, he felt more and more that I was not allowing him to give back. So, in our own minds, we were both creating a level of inequality around touch and giving that we were not communicating—mostly because we were both unaware of how deeply it was affecting us. Our rhythm had become too routine and comfortable.

Because our intentions—both internal and external—were not clear, I slowly stopped giving him massage, and he stopped offering to help me, without conscious awareness. The communication balance had broken because our intentions were not clearly expressed. Suddenly this easy-going, fantastic friendship became charged with a lot of confusion, miscommunication, and ambivalence.

In a way, I lost my sense of safety around it. Not that I ever actually felt unsafe, or that I was in any kind of danger, but there was an unease. The safety of the culture and communication that we had so carefully built between the two of us was dissolving. The nurturing warm feeling it had offered both of us was replaced with confusion, desperation, and neediness.

Second Wind

It's amazing how a connection so pure and intentional in the beginning can so easily become routine and accumulate resentment.

I looked over at the poor guy on the couch, who was now trying to engage her by showing her things on his phone.

At least I know I don't want that energy in my next relationship. I have a variety of relationships in all areas of my life that have healthy communication and touch. I am determined to keep learning how to communicate my wants and needs so others can understand and make their own decision on how they want to engage. Especially when I start dating again. There is more to be learned in this arena than I imagined, but I am really grateful I've found teachers and resources to help me expand my awareness and develop my ability to interact with touch in a more powerful way. I know it would have helped in the past and can only bring clarity to my future interactions.

I smiled to myself and reflected on my past leadership training. *I learned how to help individuals build rapport in their communities through clearer verbal and written communication, and now can adapt those tools so people can clearly communicate about touch as well.*

I glanced back toward the couch. *I hope this poor guy finds a way to get her attention and tell her what he wants and needs, too.*

My blog done, I sent it to my subscribers, closed my laptop, and threw it into my case before heading out the door.

Remedies
Adjusting Your Stride for Success

Wants and Needs

Take a moment and imagine receiving your ideal physical contact with another person. Anyone. What is your somatic sense (the sense in your body)? Does it feel relaxed? Soft? Warm? Buzzing? What happens with your breathing? Does it give you a sense of peace? Openness? Lightness? Connection? At the end of this sentence, close your eyes, imagine one scenario, and tune into that feeling. Go ahead...

Ideal touch and how it feels in the body varies among people. For example, your ideal physical contact with a coworker might be a firmer handshake, or a hand on your arm with a verbal acknowledgment that you did an amazing job. Your ideal physical contact with your sixteen-year-old son might be that he initiates a hug or a high-five. Ideally, the physical contact you receive should give you a sense of positive well-being in your body and mind, even if it is brief.

Now that you know where you want the endpoint to be and what it feels like, let's start working backwards to figure out what steps it would take to get you to that point.

One Level of Consent

How do you position yourself to express your wants and needs and maintain awareness in the moment—so that when you do get what you want, you recognize it both mentally and somatically (in the body)?

Body language is a large part (some studies say 55%) of our face-to-face communication. Imagine, as you sit here reading, that a person whom you absolutely adore and would love to hug walks toward you. (Even if you cannot think of a specific person, just imagine the sense of it.) How might you shift your body to show that you are open to giving/receiving touch? Would you sit or stand up? Smile? Open your arms? Set down whatever is in your hands? Run toward this person? Wave them forward?

Put down this book for a moment and position yourself as if they are there, right now, and feel what happens in your body. Then return to the position you were in and repeat the exercise; but, this time, pretend it is a stranger. Not someone scary, but someone you don't know well or at all. Would you change your body language or stay the same? Would you subtly close yourself off? Now, imagine what your body language would look like to open yourself again to receiving the touch you want. Take the mother in the coffee shop for example. Her body language to her son communicated "I'm busy, not now," until her desire for him to stop his disruptive behavior was stronger than her desire to continue to hold her position. Of course, we cannot all have open, welcoming body language all the time, even with the people we love, because life is life and there are things we must attend to. Perhaps if I had come into the coffee shop ten minutes earlier, I would have seen her fully engaged with her son—coloring, smiling, bending to be eye-level with him, and touching him encouragingly.

Where in your life do you turn away, cross your arms, play with your phone, turn your back, or otherwise give non-verbal signals to the people you are with that you do not want touch or engagement when you really do? And why do you think you do this? Perhaps you are feeling a bit out of sorts and want touch, but you do not want to show vulnerability so you pull out your phone as a protective mechanism. Maybe, like me with my parents on the couch, little things become a priority until the opportunity for touch has passed. Perhaps you mean to go play with your kid on the playground but start answering emails on your phone and it is suddenly time to go home; she or he has played all alone all this time while you missed an opportunity to really connect. Or maybe you are like the young female in the coffee shop. When you read that story, were you thinking that she was just completely oblivious to him? That's definitely a possibility. But it is also possible that she was fully aware of his attentiveness but did not want to (or know how to) set boundaries on touch and communication. Perhaps she had no resources to tune into what she wanted or needed, nor how to express them, and her phone was her way of managing the touch or attention demands he asked from her.

Another Level of Consent

My former husband and I had completely opposite work schedules. As I mentioned, we both were big around touch, and so when he would come home around 11 p.m. from work, I would be up waiting for him and greet him at the door with a giant hug and all the news of my day. I often felt that he would brush me off, not return my touch, or not engage with me at all. In those moments, I would feel offended and unwanted, then withdraw from communication and touch for the rest of the evening. Talking together with a coach one day, we realized what was going on. I had usually made some food, was excited to see and talk with him, and had been waiting (somewhat) patiently for him to arrive. On the other hand, he had just finished a tiring day of work, topped off by an hour-plus drive (in good weather) through Minnesota cornfields in the night. (This means there are raccoons, deer, and various other creatures popping out of nowhere onto the road to avoid, so it takes a serious level of concentration.) He would arrive at home and instead of getting five minutes to chill and breathe and reset, I'd pounce on him with enthusiasm and excitement. Once this was brought to our attention, we made an agreement that I would say "hi" but allow him time to settle in and let me know when he was ready. This improved so much in our relationship. The stories I told myself about why he did not want to touch/ communicate/ engage disappeared, he did not feel obligated to give before he was ready, and we were able to negotiate our needs and wants in a healthier way.

In chapter two I briefly mentioned a study in which two unacquainted people were to communicate emotion through a one-second touch, and that participants correctly chose some emotions, including anger, fear, and compassion over fifty percent of the time. What I did not mention about the study was that "when a woman tried to communicate anger to a man, he got zero right—he had no idea what she was doing. And when a man tried to communicate compassion to a woman, she didn't know what was going on!"[48] Men and women are wired differently when it comes to touch (and a lot of things!), and everyone has their own conditioning at play regardless of their gender so it is really important to express our wants and needs verbally as well as through body language and touch.

When I used to speak about healthy touch to women's groups, we would discuss how to connect to or include someone using touch. One example is the soccer mom sitting next to you in the stands, looking at her phone instead of watching the game. You can only guess whether she is involved in something important or doesn't feel she belongs with the rest of "the crowd" and is using the phone to protect herself. Evaluate the timing and the setting, and see if engaging through touch feels appropriate and easier than just engaging by starting a conversation. Perhaps one way to engage is to wait for an exciting or funny moment, touch her quickly but intentionally, and say, "Oh my gosh, (insert name if you know it), did you see that?" and see if you can engage her. Yes, I know I have talked incessantly about touch boundaries and asking consent. I'm not throwing it all out the window. But these are concepts to be played with. She may get startled when you first touch her, or she may fully engage and be appreciative and feel a part of the crowd, which is what I have experienced often when I use touch as an inclusion tool. Or, if that feels out of boundary for you, instead say, "Oh my gosh, did you see that? High-five!" Hold your hand up and let her make the choice. She may engage, or she may think you are crazy. But you tried in a way that felt comfortable and within your boundaries, and that is a positive step forward. And if she says *no* through body language or words, know it is not about you. You can evaluate her reaction without pushing.

Of course, it's different when we're talking about a more intimate relationship with a family member or partner. When we have a bigger stake in the relationship, asking for what we want and need can bring up self-worth issues and emotions. For example, you may feel extremely vulnerable asking your partner to sit down and take time to cuddle you on the couch when you feel sad. Perhaps you have asked in the past and heard a *no* and assume this time would elicit a *no* as well. Perhaps you were taught "only weak people need" or that "it is shameful to ask for what we want." Some of us are afraid of rejection or accusations of being oversensitive. Maybe we are waiting to find the "right" or "perfect" way to ask. Perhaps we have perceived someone to be more confident, smart, funny, or liked than us, and we have already judged ourself as less-than. If we feel they are better than us, and they do not accept our offer, then what? Sometimes we "unintentionally" sabotage an opportunity for receiving what we want because we are afraid we will get it and then we will have to adjust ourselves to the new experience. If you have resistance to asking for what you want or need, tune in and see if you can understand where it is coming from.

Consent Check-ins
Even the healthiest relationship can fall into patterns that create complacency, disconnection, or a sense of obligation. This can happen with our parents, our children, and our friends. When we stay in tune with our own needs and wants, as well as the way we self-sabotage them, we can choose to make clear agreements, communication, clarity, and synergy. We can find a way to create a balance of give-and-take that suits both sides, and check in on the agreement on occasion to make sure it still suits everyone.

One of my favorite touch agreements I had was a partnership in which I would give him a full hour (or longer) table massage monthly. In return, he'd take me out to a nice dinner. It was great because I feel special when people take me out and he felt special when I took the time and energy to bring all of my equipment home and set everything up for him like he was a real client. It was an agreement we created just to make sure we both got what we wanted and there was equality. Not that I still didn't give him little massages here and there in between, or that he wouldn't take me out for dinner if he didn't get a massage, but the intention was different (clear) and we made it special on purpose that way. It created a sense of safety, security, and boundaries that carried through into other areas of our relationship. To check in, I'd say something like, "Hey, are you up for taking me out for dinner this week if I give you a massage?" or, "Are you still up for exchanging dinner for a massage? There's this new restaurant that looks fun that I think we would both enjoy."

I urge you to occasionally check in around touch with others: your friends, your partners, and the individuals in your work, spiritual, volunteer, or even children's communities. Make sure there is comfort and safety with the level of touch you have created. See if there is room and desire for expansion or a need to alter the agreements a bit. Use this as a time to check in with yourself and your intentions. Are you touching them for them (e.g. giving them a hug because they want it and you are fine with it) or for you (e.g. you want a hug and they are fine with it), or both? We'll get into that more in chapter four, but start bringing awareness to your intention.

Did You Know?

Perhaps our desire for touch is deeper than we realize. When we stop associating touch with sex, we can also tune into the deeper needs our mind and body have. We want to interact with others and feel we belong, and touch can help us fill that need.

The hotel chain Travelodge surveyed 6,000 British adults and found 35% slept with a teddy bear. They used it to de-stress, to increase sleep, and to feel the comfort and connection to home. Fifty-one percent of British adults said they still have a teddy bear from their childhood.[49]

1,486 participants from 62 countries were asked to play a cybergame over the internet, and were led to believe they were playing with another human. As the "other" stopped interacting as often, the participants reported feeling bad and losing a sense of belonging.[50]

In a related study that used touch to mitigate feelings of loss, researchers found that affective touch, which has a pleasure or emotional component, helps reduce feelings of social exclusion. "Slow touch, which was perceived as more pleasant than fast touch, was able to buffer to a degree the effects of interpersonal threatening experiences such as ostracism... it appears that affective touch is particularly effective in reducing feelings of social exclusion."[51]

"Men shared the same bed with strangers in early American taverns, and scholarship is unearthing letters—including ones from Abraham Lincoln—revealing how men sometimes nurtured same-sex friendships that were more emotionally and physically intimate in nonsexual ways than the relationships they shared with women."[52]

"In Sweden, they found that the otherwise robust association between job strain and mortality risk disappeared among men high in social support. In fact, low levels of social support can increase the risk for premature death more than commonly known factors like smoking or alcohol consumption."[53]

"Another study found that men in relationships given a burst of oxytocin spray stood farther away from an attractive woman than men who weren't given any oxytocin. Single men didn't see any effect from the hormone, suggesting oxytocin may work as a fidelity booster for guys who are already bonded with another woman."[54]

An Internal Peek

If I asked you to choose two people with whom to communicate your touch wants and needs, who would you choose and why? What about this change could empower both you and the other?

To explore some ways to increase the amount, quality, or type of touch with people in your life, and to tune into your own wants and needs, I invite you to turn to the "Play and Explore" section for chapter three in the back of this book.

"Connection doesn't exist without giving and receiving. We need to give and we need to need."

~ Brené Brown,
American research professor ~

CHAPTER 4
YODELS & POLES
Scaling the Challenges with the 4 C's
(Curiosity, Compassion, Communication, and Commitment)

Singing to the Beat of Your Own Drum

"Bring your dancing to a close, introduce yourself to your partner, and grab one of the large mats," William, one of our two leaders, announced as he faded the music from his laptop on the table nearby. "If you want a pillow or cushion to sit on, grab one, as we will be mostly sitting for the last portion."

No more dancing?

I looked around at the other ten students who were spread out on the wooden floor of the moderate-sized yoga room. Across from us was the carpeted area, where the circle of chairs in which we had begun the class still stood. The two walls of windows in our corner allowed in the gentle rays of the evening's sunset.

I glanced at the clock hanging in the far corner. *Class is half over? That went so fast!* I smiled at the man standing in front of me, feeling how much energy I had in my body while my playful spirit beamed from my eyes. We had just spent the last thirty minutes connecting with our bodies through dance, really tuning into our internal sensations, as William led us through a variety of music and playful prompts. Now it was time to start the partnering portion of the workshop focused on our relationship to touch.

"I'm Dawn," I said and held my hand out for a shake.

"Hi, Dawn. I'm Alan," he said, looking into my eyes and chuckling as his hand met mine. "Nice to meet you."

"You too," I replied before turning and walking with him to the wall to grab a mat. "I wonder what we're doing next."

I feel really comfortable with him and the people here. The way Claire and William create a sense of safety and connection through their leadership is so amazing.

We laid out the mat and sat down, legs crossed, facing each other.

When everyone looked settled, William began the instruction. "You will sit on the opposite ends of the mats, and your job is to be aware of the thoughts in your mind and the sensations in your body—to learn how it feels when you are comfortable or uncomfortable, and what it feels like you want to do in response to those thoughts and sensations. At each stage, I want each of you to feel into your body and mind and see if you desire to move closer together, stay at the same distance, or move further apart. The person with the longest hair is going to be the 'caller,' and the person with the shorter hair will be the 'callee.' When prompted, the 'caller' can choose to gesture their partner closer, hold their hand up to ask them to stay, or gesture them back. The 'callee' gets to feel into his or her body and make their own decision. However, the person who wants the most space has priority. 'Callee,' if you are prompted to move back, please do so; and if you are prompted to stay, you can decide whether to stay or move back. I will give a series of prompts, and please do not gesture or move before I instruct. I will tell you before the last instruction. If you wish, at that time, you may touch each other on the arms however you both choose and use words to communicate quietly." William looked around the room for understanding. "I'll keep guiding you through it, so just listen to my instructions as we go," he finished. "If you have any questions, please raise your hand."

I totally want touch. I thought, as I remembered how disconnected and lonely I felt before the dancing section of the class. *No question about it.* I felt the raw need for connection in my core. *Okay, so tuning in, I'm clear. I'm looking forward to being touched.* The room settled in as the last wisps of sunlight left the room, leaving us lit only by the soft, yellow can lights above.

"Take a few deep breaths and center yourself," William started, "tuning into your body and your current sensations. What does it feel like to be on your own right now—the other person on the other side of the mat?" He paused.

I watched Alan from my side of the mat, watching his face and his breath, curious about his thoughts. *I'm feeling anxious in a hurry-up kind of way.* I took a deep breath and tried to be patient.

"Would you like the person to be closer to you, with the possibility of touching eventually?" William guided.

"Caller, if you would like your partner to move forward, you may gesture so now. Callee, you get to also decide if you want to stay where you are or move forward for now. Please only move forward about six inches if you choose to do so."

I gestured, and after a brief pause, Alan moved forward about six inches. I let out a breath. *Huh, I didn't realize I was holding that. I guess I was a bit nervous he wouldn't move forward. There's still a couple feet between us and time for him to make that decision.* A sinking sensation crept in at the thought.

"Everyone, tune in again and re-evaluate. How does it feel now that you are in the new position? If your partner chose not to move, remember they are honoring themselves and their current needs. Maybe this is the first time that they have been able to say *no* to moving closer to someone, and this is a powerful moment for them."

Oh yeah. I almost forgot that some people want to learn to say no and create more boundaries around touch, rather than just going for it like I always do. I stifled a giggle at myself.

"And if your default is to say *yes* to touch, perhaps play with saying *no* for once and see how it feels," he continued, as if he had read my mind.

Nope, not today. "The resistance is strong with this one," my internal comedian joked, probably getting the *Star Wars* quote completely wrong. *I may not practice my no much, but dang it, I am really clear on what I want right now.* William continued having us feel into our bodies before allowing another prompt, reminding us all of our ability and strength to communicate what we wanted, trusting our partner would take care of him/herself. I gestured Alan forward again and, after another breath, he moved forward six inches.

I looked into his eyes, and allowed myself to connect that way. *I do need to practice connecting without touch and without feeling like someone will take it sexually,* I reminded myself, and allowed my face and body to soften from one of "caller in charge" to "open to connection." *It seems I was creating a boundary through my body language. I'll have to be more aware of that in the future.*

Alan met my gaze, and we watched each other as William repeated the same instructions in a slightly different way again, encouraging us to honor our boundaries if it felt right, push them if we were ready, or try something new. "Making your choice consciously on how you want to proceed, callers, you may now choose your gesture," he finished.

I'm feeling a bit vulnerable that he will stop moving closer, I noticed as I gestured him forward again. *Interesting.* He moved forward again, and now we were within touching distance if we both extended our arms. *It feels really comfortable and easy. My body feels relaxed, still a bit anticipatory in a good way, but it's softened.*

"Remember, if the person has kept a distance or increased it, note how that is in your body, as well as honor that their decision has nothing to do with you—it's all about finding power in their own choice."

Well, I'm glad he hasn't made that choice, but I think at this point, I would be okay if he did. I feel connected through our gaze. We continued to watch each other, as I scanned for any unnoticed feelings or body sensations. *I feel pretty grounded and clear.*

"This will be the last prompt, so if you wish to practice creating distance, do so, and if you want to create physical contact, you may also do so. Please remember to use as few words as possible, but if you need to use them to communicate, do so quietly so you don't disturb anyone around you." William's gentle words floated through the room, as people made their final decisions.

I gestured Alan forward, and he moved so our knees were touching. I reached my hands out, palm up, and he laid his hands on mine. I felt my body soften even more as my breath deepened. *Really? I was still holding my breath? Wow. Now what are we supposed to do? I suppose technically I'm still the lead.* I moved my hands so they were on top of his, then up his forearm, and stopped as my hands rested on his elbow and he turned his palms up.

"For those of you who are touching, feel free to communicate your touch boundaries, anywhere on your arms from the shoulder down. You can limit it to hands, forearms, upper arms—whatever the person with the strongest boundaries desires," William instructed. "Be present with your touch though. Feel what it is like to give and receive touch. If something has even a hint of being uncomfortable, if it is something you do not want, pause and communicate with your partner. That can mean the boundaries change, that the touch is light and tickles, that the touch is too fast and you can't feel inside. Regardless of what comes up, both of you stay present and communicate."

"I'm good with it all," I said, smiling and watching his face.

"Me too," he chuckled, as we started slowly started mindfully moving our hands over each other's forearms, feeling into the sensation. He squeezed down my arms, and I smiled.

"That's awesomeness," I said, using one of my favorite "I don't know if it's a word" words. My arms were sore from too many massages, and I immediately dropped my arms on my lap to allow the full experience. *That feels amazing. It does remind me though, I should really get a massage this week.* I sighed as the tension left my arms and he brushed his hands off of mine. *We can work up to the shoulders? Let's see if I can do this comfortably.* I leaned forward and reached my hands up to his shoulders. With a firm pressure, I slowly brushed down his arm and forearm.

"Play with different kinds of touch. You can stay still, move quickly, use fingertips, arm against arm, whatever feels good to the two of you," William prompted.

Alan and I looked at each other, smiled, and immediately became playful with our touch. *I'm going to tickle his forearms like my nephews tickle mine. Ha! Funny, he just started using his fingertips too, although he's being much firmer than I am. This is super fun.* I started watching where my hands were going, reached my left forearm up, intending to go for his shoulder, and he lifted his as well, and we fell into touching forearm to forearm. *This reminds me of the old martial arts exercises,* I thought as I rolled my arm over his, keeping contact the whole time as our arms moved in counterbalance. *It's like two birds swooping around each other in the air, except touching,*

I thought, giggling at my own internal dialogue. *It feels so free though.*

We kept playing with our touch, switching arms eventually and catching each other's eye to affirm things were still comfortable until William gently interrupted. "And now, no matter where you ended up with your partner, acknowledge the roles you each played, and the 'callee' will move slowly back to their original point, six inches at a time. Do it on your own time, but both take a moment to feel into your body between every movement. What does it feel like to have more distance between the two of you? Is it more comfortable or less? What happens in your body? What is your reaction? Make sure you leave enough time to really pause at each step and notice." Silence filled the room again as partners began the process of separation.

Alan smiled again and we met eyes as we took our hands off each other. He gave a little nod, and moved back six inches.

Immediately overcome, I gasped audibly as a wave of emotion hit me and tears rolled down my face. *It's like he took my heart and ripped it out of my chest. Why am I suddenly in so much pain?* Understanding hit me in a second wave. *All I've been doing for the last nine months is making connections and then leaving. Creating friendships and then transitioning away. I've just always had somewhere new and fun to go, so I didn't realize how much the lack of deeper connection had hurt me. No wonder I've been so touch-needy. I haven't healed from all the disconnection, including the nine months away from my friends and family.*

He looked at me, kindness and empathy in his eyes, and moved back another six inches. The silent tears kept coming as he continued to slowly move back, pausing at each step, watching me and honoring my pain though the whole process. *At least he doesn't look freaked out by my sudden emotion and he's maintaining a level of connection. That's really helpful.* The wave over, and peace washing over me finally, we took a few deep breaths together.

"When you are finished, we will take a quick break." William stood up and stretched as he gave the final instructions. "Feel free to move around, use the bathroom, grab snacks, and do whatever you need for self-care. We will come back together in fifteen minutes."

I stood up, finally wiping the tears off my face, grabbed my water bottle from my chair, and walked to the bathroom. *I feel really good about that. And, I've come a long way being able to cry in public.*

I stood in line for the only bathroom and chatted casually with a few of the participants before returning to the warmly lit yoga room. I was grabbing a couple of raspberries and chocolate covered almonds from the table when Claire announced the end of the break.

Dang, that was fast. I don't think I've actually processed anything yet. I checked in really quick. *I feel normal—*

whatever that means. I giggled to myself as I realized that what I considered "normal" in my body would be completely strange and foreign to another. *Yep. There is no normal, especially with me.* I tried to put on my serious, business-like persona to ground myself again. *Whatever. You are learning about boundaries and saying no. That also means you get to say no to suppressing the childish, playful part of yourself.* Even though I was clear it was my internal comedian talking, I heeded the advice, took a deep breath, and walked back to the mat.

"Welcome back," William started. "Are there any questions?" He paused for a bit, waiting for us to gain courage or formulate a question, before he continued. "We will go through the same procedure, switching roles..."

Alan is now the 'caller,' and I am 'callee,' I reminded my brain to let go, as William talked us through the same process until Alan and I were touching once again.

Our touch started playfully, again, as I purposefully engaged in a way that didn't feel like I was trying to give, the way I did in massage sessions. It was a much easier round, and we separated at the end of it without another emotional upheaval on my part. *It's interesting that I felt so much peace on this round,* I mused, *I wonder if I released most of the struggle before, or if I feel more in control being the 'callee,' assuming correctly he was going to call me in every time. Maybe it's just because this time I knew the end was going to be to separate, whereas the first time I thought the end was the coming together.*

After a group share of our experience and the closing announcements from Claire, Alan put away our mat while I drifted over to the table to grab a few more chocolate covered almonds and chat with the people already gathered there. A few minutes later, I noticed Alan looking at the class and retreat list and walked over to him.

"Are you coming to the next class?" I asked, curious about his experience tonight and his future plans with the group. "I signed up for the next few before I head back to Europe."

"I don't think I can make them," he replied. "I'm heading to Peru in a couple weeks for a mission trip, and it's getting really busy with all the preparation. I'm going to talk to Claire about this weekend thing though." He gestured to the upcoming weekend retreat that I had attended the previous year.

"I went to that last year," I said, "and found it really valuable…" I thought about sharing more, but wasn't sure how to put my experience into words, knowing that everyone there had taken something different out of it. "If tonight fit you, I think you would really enjoy it."

"Yeah, but I might have a conflict then," he said vaguely. "I'd have to really negotiate some stuff to make the whole weekend."

"Well, I'd go again," I said wistfully, wishing I also didn't have a conflict that weekend. *A whole weekend of connection like tonight would be really amazing in* my life right now. But time is short, and I have a lot of obligations to meet before I leave again.*

He turned to me. "Maybe if you're up for it, we could meet for coffee and you could share more about your experience?"

I cocked my head, suddenly curious. *Is he asking for guidance, wanting to learn about boundaries and communication, knowing I've done this? Or is he asking me out?* I didn't want to jump to any conclusion, and I definitely wasn't going to start dating before going to Europe again. *That was a hot mess, and we weren't even serious.* I came back to the present as quickly as I left it. *He seems sincere, and what harm can an exchange of numbers do? I can feel him out more over the phone and clarify any boundaries if needed. It will be a good practice for learning to say* no *if I decide to or need to later.*

We exchanged numbers. I told him I'd call as soon as I got in front of my planner in about an hour, and I headed out into the dark, chilly night for the comfort of home.

As I drove the familiar route home, I reflected on the impact of that first separation.

I can't believe how deeply I felt that. I'm amazed at how important connection is to me. I feel it so intensely, like that time I joined the ecstatic dance group with Jon.

Listening to the Echo

"There are only a few rules while dancing here," Kari, the leader, addressed the big circle of dancers. "One, dance however you want without judgment and without judging others. You can run, skip, jump, make vocalizations, spin, lay down, roll around on the floor, rest on the edges, or whatever you feel called to do that honors your needs and takes care of you. Two, no words may be spoken during dance. All communication should be done using gestures and touch. Three, some people enjoy dancing for a while with others. You can communicate you want to dance with someone, and wait for them to nod or invite you into his or her space. If you do not want to dance with somebody and they attempt to dance with you, it is okay and encouraged to just bow out. Remember, bowing out is an individual taking care of themselves and their body in the moment, and not a reflection upon you in any way. Do not take it personally."

Those are great rules. I wish it had been that easy in my twenties at the dance clubs! I gazed around the circle at the variety of people sitting in the open wooden-floored meeting space inside the small Texan church. *This is going to be a lot of fun.*

Kari prompted everyone to declare an intention for the session, and the variety of answers surprised me. They ranged from an intention to be playful to an intention to heal oneself and let go of body stress through movement. The DJ stepped behind the table as the circle broke and people stood up, and then the music started with a steady rhythm that was easy to feel and move to. I stood with my eyes closed, getting a sense of the beat, the energy of the music, and how I wanted to start dancing. Slower at first, allowing myself to get grounded, to feel my breath, and to remind myself to just be playful and explore.

You don't know this music, but you know how to move and how to dance and how to feel free, I told myself. *Just do what you would do in your kitchen.*

The music progressed into faster yet more melodic songs, rhythms changing gradually with each one. There were no words—just a variety of tones and instruments—but the energy remained. This music inspired the body to dance.

I remember spinning around the edges of the group, seeing the cacti in the garden outside through the windows, and feeling my hair and my long skirt fly around me as I giggled like a small child. It was pure freedom, and I was high on the knowledge that other people around me were feeling the same. I knew I wanted to connect with people; but as I tried to catch someone's eye to get permission or make a connection, no one seemed to respond. They all seemed like they were engaging with each other, but leaving me isolated.

Is it because I don't know anyone? Are people only dancing with those they know? Or maybe I sent a message that I don't want to dance with anyone else because of what I said?

My mind scrambled for reasons why no one would connect, as I fought off subtle feelings of rejection, despite Kari's instructions. Within a few short minutes, boredom and apathy overtook me, and I blamed it on the new song playing. I kept dancing by myself, forgetting briefly about my intention to be playful, until the music overtook me and I released the self-imposed burden of separation. Some people would dance very close but not really engage physically or with their eyes, which felt normal, as if they were just doing their thing. Other people would come near, look at me, do something a little playful, and then dance away.

This is super fun, I decided, and how nice to be in a safe space dancing, where I don't have to guard against guys touching me inappropriately or hitting on me. I feel so playful when others interact briefly and so joyfully.

I felt myself becoming lighter and freer in my body and in my dancing, a huge contrast to the bored feeling I had when people "ignored" me.

Perhaps all the boredom was a deeper protection mechanism that helped shield me from feeling needy, ignored, or unwanted? I pondered this for a moment as I continued dancing, still trying to find an area where people wanted to engage, but not feeling so desperate about it. Suddenly, I noticed myself needing my own space and feeling almost claustrophobic, as if it had become too much for my body and mind to be engaged with so many swaying, swirling, bouncy people.

I tuned into my body and felt an internal sluggishness and weight in some spots, and it made me feel really restless.

I'm dancing. How on earth can I feel restless right now? What is all this movement and touch/no touch fluidity doing to me? I was so curious, even as I was feeling inundated with input.

The music finally came to a close, and Kari prompted us to form a closing circle. "Thank you everyone for coming. If anyone wants to share an experience, thoughts, or whatever is in your mind, feel free to do so."

One woman spoke up immediately. "I just want to apologize for turning down so many invitations to dance. I just really needed to be in my own space today."

"I want to appreciate the people who came near me today. It felt so lovely to be a part of such a caring and respectful group. I feel I don't get that much in my daily life," another shared.

Comments continued like popcorn, with many people expressing an experience of healing, love, gratitude, or connection in some way that was deeper than a conversation could be. For many, being able to move in and out of touch with others was powerful.

Poles Provide Balance During Rocky Communication

It was the first time I had really heard people expressing such intense feelings around dancing, and it impacted the way I chose to interact with others in groups from then on. What a powerful way for me to learn that an intention to be connected works beyond the levels of touch and speech. Feeling connected is also about being acknowledged wherever we are in our process.

I pulled into the driveway of my childhood home, grateful for all of the experiences that were helping me deepen my ability to connect through touch and in so many other ways. Smiling, I parked the car, walked into the house, gave my parents a hug, and called it a night.

I don't know where all of this will go with Alan, but I do know that I have enough awareness and tools now to make it a healthy experience.

The thought made me smile again as I drifted off to sleep.

But a week later, as I followed Alan's grey, four-door car to the coffee shop in the darkness, the questions started. *Are we just talking about class? He mentioned he was interested? Or is this a date?*

We had been communicating all week, and a lot that day, trying to get our schedules to work together. I felt good about my commitment to stick to my other priorities, and I felt great about the easy communication that had happened between us.

I pulled into a parking space next to his. *My intention is for this to just be a continuation of touch communication. To be able to clearly feel whatever I feel, and to communicate if I feel something is happening I do not want.* Feeling a bit of excitement to have something to do besides work this evening, I stepped out of the car and walked into the shop with him.

I watched him take in the atmosphere—cozy couches and bright art in the open space. *I hope he likes it as much as I do.* The baristas were high-energy and smiley for 9:30 p.m., and I grabbed a warm tea. *I really want a white chocolate Americano, but would prefer to fall asleep before 3 a.m.* As Alan was ordering, I looked around and eyed up the open couch.

"Where should we sit?" he asked, looking around.

"How about the couch over there?" I gestured, pointing to the oversized brown couch the teens had occupied the week before. *I would love to sit in something comfortable and just relax and spread out.*

"Looks great." We walked over and I sat in the corner of the couch, turned sideways, kicked one sandal off, and tucked my foot under me. He sat next to me and set his tea on the long, low wooden table in front of us.

"So," I started, ready to jump into conversation and learn more about this guy, "before I start asking you a million questions, I feel really comfortable with you after class the other night. Are you still comfortable with touching outside of class? I tend to touch with my hands while I talk. Can I touch you while we talk, or would you prefer some space?"

"I'm comfortable with touch," he said. "You seem like a kind and open person."

"Cool," I said, a bit proud that I had the awareness to ask instead of assume. *I'm getting better at being clear in my communication.*

"What did you think about class? Are you going to go to any of the others? Did you sign up for the weekend or did it end up being a conflict?"

He paused and thought for a bit. "That was the first class I've been to, and it was interesting." He reflected, collecting his thoughts. "I talked to Claire and the people from my trip about the weekend, but it's not going to work this time around. Things are moving very fast with these trips, and it will take up quite a bit of time and energy to prepare." He paused again.

He thinks through his words carefully, I noticed. *I better be careful not to talk over him. I guess I can work on that bad habit since I don't have to be as concerned about touch boundaries.*

"You seemed passionate about it when you mentioned it that night. Tell me about it." He took a sip of his tea, watching me with curiosity.

"Well," I paused. "The core lesson was tuning into our bodies so we can practice honoring both mental cues and physical cues of our own boundaries of physical contact. They led us through a series of exercises to help us really tune into our core sensations, teaching us to say *yes* and *no* or at least *pause* when we were doing the exercises. Expressing what we want and do not want in a safe environment was a huge piece as well."

As I talked, I touched his knee or upper arm to emphasize points, and I was grateful for the ease that had been created through our communication. Our conversations unfolded easily, eventually moving on to delicate subjects like religion and spirituality.

"I think I'm going to write a book about touch," I mentioned hesitantly, not sure what his reaction would be. "I feel it's so important for people to be able to bring touch back into their lives in a healthy way that aligns with their values."

"Oh my gosh! You're going to write a book?" The curiosity and joy in his voice was refreshing.

"One of the things I'd like to do is help people heal their fears or restrictions around physical contact that maybe were religious at the base but don't align well with their current beliefs or don't serve them in their relationships. I believe, and science is proving, that physical contact is such a big part of building trust in our networks. The trick, of course, is helping people to understand and heal the unhealthy patterns that have been set by cultural and/or religious conditioning and traumatic touch experiences, including our culture's insistence that sex is always part of touch."

Alan looked up, obviously deep in thought, so I paused to give him an opportunity to process and respond. "Yes," he said a bit hesitantly, "I know that what I'm taught in my church is not always in alignment with what I have observed when it comes to touch. I've done quite a bit of research; and I know some cultures see touch as an everyday part of life with members of society, and others see it purely as sexual." He headed back into his own brain for a bit.

I kept quiet, really practicing my talking boundaries. It was so safe, in fact, that I had subconsciously snuggled in a little bit more. My knee was now touching his leg and hip, and it felt completely natural. The more we connected through verbal communication, the more natural the touch communication became as well. It wasn't sexual or charged—it was just like I would sit with my sister or with my dad or a very close friend.

These ideas for my book might actually work! I giggled. *I've been putting the theory into practice, but it's nice to see that the more skill I acquire, and the easier these things become, the more awareness I have around the impact that it's making in my own communities and cultures.*

Suddenly, I noticed the baristas doing their final sweep, picking up and cleaning under chairs.

"Oh my gosh, I don't want this conversation to be over, but it looks like they are cleaning up. We should probably head out," I said, disappointed but aware of how late it actually was.

"I know," he said smiling, "time went fast. It's so great to learn so much from each other."

"Well, I will be in your neighborhood next Saturday morning visiting my friend Evelyn. Perhaps when she has to leave to go meet her boys, you and I could go to the park and hike? I'll even let you talk more next time!" I joked, realizing how much I had really gone on about my passions.

He laughed. "That sounds great." We stood up, thanked the baristas, and walked out of the coffee shop together.

"Let me know what time next Saturday when you know," he said. "I'll see you then."

"Perfect." We exchanged a hug and jumped into our own cars and waved goodbye.

I wish all of my relationships were as simple as this one feels. So many of my other relationships have required me to do all of the reaching out.

As I drove home, I thought about the last experience that had left a bad taste in my mouth.

Accepting Slippery Slopes with Compassion

"Are you coming to the baby shower on Saturday?" Angela asked me as she scurried by the front desk to grab some papers.

"Baby shower? I didn't know one was happening?" I was stunned.

I knew she was pregnant, but not one person has mentioned the shower to me. It feels like they don't make any effort to include me. I don't even know when the meetings are anymore.

"Yeah, I thought you knew. Anyway, I think it got shared on our Facebook group, so you can go there and get details. Noon to three at Veronica's house."

"I can't make it. I already have other plans." I tried to keep my tone light as the disappointment and sense of isolation hit me hard.

If they wanted me there anyway, someone would have said something by now, right? I really thought I would have a better experience in this environment.

I had been welcomed to the team with open arms, and I was so glad to be in an environment where people were so genuinely expressive and used physical contact naturally. However, I had quickly noticed that if I didn't make an active effort to reach out and connect, no one else would. At first, I assumed it was because I was new and getting to know people. Then I wondered if my feelings were just residuals from the shaming incident, making me feel like an outsider again. Finally, I realized that while the women were easy with touch, hugs, and physical connection, they were not great at verbal communication and updates outside of the meetings. So if the group scheduled outings or made plans to connect, and I wasn't present at the meeting, rarely did someone reach out to include me. I resorted to asking the receptionist to fill me in or looking at the sign-up sheet posted on the employee wall. Even when I asked around to see what others were doing after work, they were busy or had plans one-on-one with each other, or had an excuse not to schedule something for the following week. I felt I was always making the effort, and after being turned down enough and not being reached out to, I had just become tired of it. Once I stopped actively trying, the isolation increased exponentially, and I seemed to be left out of everything, even the baby showers.

Commitment to the Path

Yes, that experience taught me that being connected takes intention and communication on everyone's part. I know that next time, if I choose to work there when I return from Europe, I will need to communicate my needs better. No matter what space I end up in, if there are others around, I know now the level of communication I want to uphold in order to take care of my needs and try to make a more impactful connection with the community I work within. This experience with Alan tonight reminded me of how much easier this can be than I've made it before.

I was really proud of myself as I went to bed that night and excited to meet up with this genuinely lovely soul again the next week.

Fortunately, the week passed quickly thanks to tons of massage appointments and preparations for Europe, and it seemed like no time at all before I met him at the park for a hike.

"Well," Alan started, looking around the local urban park, "let's start walking on that trail over there." He pointed toward a small lake and forested area.

"Looks great," I agreed, falling into step with him and noticing the air smelled of lakes and fresh-cut grass. "How was your week?"

We walked and talked about what he was going to be doing on his trips, his hesitations and excitements, and even my experiences with mission/volunteer trips in other countries and what I had learned about different cultures. Eventually the culture conversation turned back to touch, and I told him about an experiential touch-learning game I had practiced with my coach, Claire.

"It's called the 3-Minute Game and there's a woman, Dr. Betty Martin, who has a lot of information about it on her website," I started. "It helps people gain self-awareness of different aspects of touch in different situations and teaches them where they are with consent. In fact, she has a whole wheel that helps you identify where you are with your consent levels. I've only played it once, and as someone who thought I was really aware of touch, this game brought me to a whole other level. For example..." I continued sharing about some of the realizations I'd had.

"Wow, it sounds like it really helps refine a sense of what you enjoy and how to really be aware when you are not allowing yourself to receive," he replied thoughtfully and then laughed. "It actually sounds kind of fun."

"Well, the game itself is really simple. It's just four rounds of three minutes each. Each round, we have a different role, so we give and receive three minutes of touch twice each—one time focused on giving, one time focused on receiving for each role. I've watched all the videos on it, plus played it the one time. We can try if you want?"

He nodded affirmatively, and we found a simple backless bench off the side of the trail on the edge of the park where we sat straddling it, facing each other.

"Okay. The game is simple. Same rules as class: Tune into yourself, don't do anything you don't want, and don't allow me to do anything that you don't like. Communication is key, as well as feeling inside yourself and your reactions in every moment."

"Okay," he said. "How do we start?"

"One person asks for what they want for touch for three minutes, and the other gives it. The one receiving touch can and should make adjustments throughout, finding ways to make it even better for themselves—harder, lighter, faster, slower, different area, use a different part to touch, and so on. If the receiver is not directing enough, the giver should pause to have them tune in. We can keep the touch areas to head, neck, arms, shoulders, and hands, so we can really focus and refine. The giver checks in the whole time to make sure it is comfortable in every way. For example, if I ask for harder pressure and it would bother your hands to do so, you would tell me *no,* and I would adjust my request. At the end of three minutes, we switch roles. Make sense?"

"Yep," he said, "I'll give first."

I set my phone for three minutes and asked him to massage my thumb and hand on my right side, having him adjust pressure and move up my arm a bit, then switch to tractioning my left hand from my arm, and tickling the underside of my forearm with his fingernails.

When I played this before, I had a hard time asking for so many adjustments because I'd just sink into the feeling and forget that I was trying to play with what might make it even better.

The timer interrupted my thoughts. "Okay, your turn. How would you like me to touch you for three minutes?" I reset the timer as he thought.

He had me start by tickling his arms, and asked me to massage his head with my fingers. I stood up and walked behind him to make it comfortable for myself—part of the lesson of making sure that I was taking care of myself, even while giving. Then he asked for some pressure on his shoulders to help stretch and relax them.

The giving part feels easy, but I can tell sometimes I don't want him to direct. I want to finish an area or do more in a spot before changing it up. I guess it can be hard to give purely for someone else, as our own ideas of what feels good or is right can get in the way.

The timer went off again, and I stopped and sat back down in front of him. "What do you think?"

"Yeah, that part was fun. Three minutes goes way too fast though," he chuckled. "But you mentioned four rounds, so do we do the same thing again?"

"Kind of. So, in that round, we acted strictly as giving/receiving, which we do a lot in our daily lives in different ways. We go to a restaurant and get served by a waiter. A kid asks for a kiss on an owie and we kiss it. Someone asks for a hug and we give it. We take the garbage out for our mom, bring someone a gift, give someone a compliment, or cook dinner for a friend. All those can be examples of doing an action that is a benefit or a gift to the other person—no strings attached. But let's say you cook me dinner and you put moldy cheese in it. I hate moldy cheese and sometimes it makes me gag. But I eat it, endure it, and tolerate it instead of telling you I cannot eat it because of the cheese. Now your gift to me *isn't* being received as a gift. I have fallen outside of consent. I have not told you that I don't eat moldy cheese, so I force myself to do it—it's a form of non-consent. We do this all the time around touch, especially. We endure touch we do not want, and thus negate the gift the other person is giving us."

"You know, my married friends share a lot about enduring touch. I know a guy whose wife told him—*after twenty years of marriage*—that she hated it when he held the back of her neck. Isn't that amazing?" he asked incredulously. "Like, what else isn't being shared in the relationship? What else is the other tolerating?"

I thought about that for a moment, reflecting on some of my friends' complaints over the years, and then gave him the best answer I could find in that moment: "Maybe she liked it some days and not others but couldn't clarify within herself and didn't communicate on the days she needed something different. Or maybe she thought she told him and just wasn't clear. Maybe he couldn't hear it for some reason. I know I've done that in relationships in the past."

"There are definitely a lot of variables. And, of course, I only heard one side. But it does seem like everyone communicating sooner rather than later would make the whole relationship smoother and prevent so much building up and spilling over into other areas." He mulled that over for a brief moment. "Okay, so what else?"

"In this next round, when I touch you, instead of the intention being to touch you for *your* enjoyment, my intention is to find how *I* can feel the most enjoyment while touching you."

"Like when people ask my bald friend if they can feel his head?" he asked, laughing. "Poor guy gets that a lot."

"Yep. If the person touching is enjoying it and it's within consent for your friend, then each of them is playing one of the roles. Another example is the enjoyment of feeling the soft fur of a cat, who will leave if he or she doesn't like it."

He thought intently for a few seconds. "I suppose there are many ways we do it subconsciously, but it sounds so weird to phrase it as 'taking enjoyment by touching another.'"

"Yeah, but I'm not good at explaining the concepts yet either," I warned. "Remember, this is only my second time playing." I continued the instructions as I understood them. "Your intention, as the person receiving the touch, is to monitor yourself and your sensations as well. The intention of my touch isn't to have you enjoy it. However, it shouldn't be uncomfortable in any way for you physically, mentally, or emotionally. You *must* pause or stop me if it feels like you are enduring in any way. As you allow me to find good sensations in my hands by touching you, it is also a disservice to yourself and me to allow me to do something that you don't like. It is outside of consent, which is what we are trying to learn more about." I paused for a bit to let that concept sink in. "For example, when I played this before and I was the person touching, it was harder for me to create a sense of my own physical enjoyment instead of giving to the other person. I kept jumping into a role where I was doing for her instead of for myself. She would feel that and check in with me: 'Are you doing that for me or for you?' I learned I had a hard time feeling and accepting what she was giving back. I wasn't allowing her gift of being present for me to give me joy. I kept pushing it away mentally and trying to give to her instead."

"I think I've got it," he said as he closed his eyes and relaxed, a soft smile on his face. "Go for it."

I started the timer, stood up, and started gently moving my hands and then forearms over the top of his hair, my intention to allow his hair to tickle my skin and get my senses reset from the 'giving' to 'receiving' mode.

Dang, this is still hard, even with someone I'm so comfortable with. My years of giving with massage therapy allows me to tune in fast, and even feel the sensations in my hands and arms, but I quickly feel like I run out of things to do.

I attempted to focus and relax, and just allow myself to be playful. I continued from his hair onto his face, curious how the smoothness of his skin or the hair on his face would feel.

Aha, maybe.... I knelt next to the bench, took his arm, and draped it over my shoulder, as if he was resting his arm on me. *That feels cozy, but maybe I can receive this easily because it feels more reciprocal.* Just as I removed his arm and tried to figure out how else to sense beyond using my hands, the alarm broke the silence.

I sat down, almost glad to be done with this portion. "Your turn." I reset the alarm and closed my eyes, curious what he would do.

I felt him stand and start lightly skimming his hands over the tops of my shoulders, over my hair, and around my face. He picked up my hand and smoothed the back of it over his own face, then used my fingers to tickle his arm and hand.

I stifled a giggle as I remembered how my partner had tested my *no* on purpose during our training. She was running her hands over my face, then stuck her fingers in my ear and left them there. I was surprised, and it took me about five seconds to tell her I didn't like her fingers in my ears and to please choose something different.

She made her point though, I thought right before the timer beeped again.

Alan sat back down as I opened my eyes and turned the obnoxious thing off.

"What do you think?" I inquired quickly, wanting him to share before I started babbling again. "What did you feel or learn or whatever?"

He laughed. "It was really interesting. I can see why the game is so valuable. Like, when you were running your hands over my face, I could feel they were a bit sticky from the heat. And I knew I didn't like the feeling of the stickiness," he said slowly and paused, watching my face for my reaction. "At the same time the touch was nice, so it wasn't bad, it just wasn't as enjoyable as before. But it was about you, so I had a hard time deciding if I was tolerating, or if was just a different sensation."

"You didn't stop me, so was it okay?" I asked a bit embarrassed but also interested in his discovery.

Ugh, and the word okay *is like* fine. *It doesn't really clarify whether consent is happening. It has more of an implication of endurance or tolerance than consent.*

"I don't feel anything bad or negative about it, and the sensation was gone as soon as you stopped touching my face. I guess it wasn't long enough for me to truly know."

"Yeah, it's deeper than it seems at first. You can have a ton of 'aha' moments by playing this with different people and expanding where you can touch on the body." I laughed. "At least that's what my teachers tell me."

"Did they address how our culture often has a hard time giving and receiving touch?" he asked, making the connection back to the topic of conversation at the coffee shop.

"A bit. I think many people in our culture have moments where we get uncomfortable and feel like we don't deserve what we are given—like we have to give back or do more for the other in order to feel good or to be liked."

It's fun to be with someone just as intentional around touch. I wonder if I played with someone who wasn't so introspective, if more old feelings would have come up. I'm so sensitive to energy that I can easily tell when others aren't aware, and I can become uneasy or irritated quickly.

I thought back to the ten-day silent retreat, where I really learned to tune into my body sensations as I learned about acceptance and awareness.

Cleansing Waterfalls

I sat cross-legged on my cushion in the large open hall with about 100 other people. We had been organized into neat rows, women on the right, men on the left, all facing the front where the two teachers—one male and one female—sat. We were all silent, listening to the steady, deep voice of Mr. S.N. Goenka coming through speakers and giving instructions. Some of us were just listening; others were already deep into their fourth day of meditation.

Of course, I was having trouble focusing because "By and Down the River," by the band A Perfect Circle, was rolling through the back of my head, as it had been for days.

"Allow it to be," my teacher had said when I confessed that three days of breathing and silence made me feel tortured day and night. "Do not run from it, nor move toward something else. Just notice it and accept it, the way you are learning with your body sensations."

I know this is my brain sending me a message about whatever I'm processing. The outer voice stopped and silence descended over the room. I took a breath and brought my attention to the top of my head.

"Piece by piece... diligently... patiently. Have perfect equanimity... don't crave pleasant sensation... don't react with aversion to uncomfortable sensation." Goenka's measured voice resonated, as I started scanning down my back. "Every sensation you experience should help you develop your equanimity."

I have definitely spent a long time trying to avoid pain and run toward pleasure. Even with my level of self-awareness. I scanned my whole body slowly, stopping to observe spots I couldn't feel any sensation, where it felt blank or empty. *My belly feels so relaxed and strong, while at the same time I can feel that tension happening in my right hip again. It's all the hiking followed by all the sitting.* I observed the pain, knowing that moving away from it can interrupt the potential release of whatever I was storing there emotionally. *All things change, pleasure and pain, so allow, soften into it, and then move on,* I reminded myself.

"Showing only bits and pieces/'Til the tide betrays you and your empty allocution..." A Perfect Circle blared in my head, and I felt my chest tighten and my breath become shallow.

Observe, breathe, allow. This is the part that's hard. Not the ten days without talking. I could feel my emotions coming in waves as my brain flooded memories and images into my awareness. *Bring your attention back to your breath.* I sat with it as the emotions and visuals of past relationships washed over me. Regret, sorrow, loneliness. The wave passed, and I brought my attention back to my hip and kept scanning. *These emotions and sensations have become more frequent and stronger over the last day. I really regret the way it ended with James. I am more hurt than I thought. Over and over, I've just given with unawareness, with unspoken expectation.* I could feel my chest and throat tighten more and more as my breath became shallow. *Don't run, sit with the sensation. Be present, focus on sensation to clear the mind.*

It's all your fault, you know. Your failed marriage, your inability to hold onto a relationship. You even over-gave to your business. You didn't communicate your needs to James. You allowed your 'give' to override your needs. My critical ego jumped in.

Sadness washed over me, as tears suddenly rolled down my face and I dropped my head to cry. *I could get up and go out of the room, but this feels like it will pass quickly. And I'm not the first one to cry in here, for sure.* The wave passed almost as suddenly as it came, as I took a breath, and focused in again on my body. *Well, the song's quiet again for a while, my hip feels really soft. No pain at all.* I noted this with relief, as I continued to scan down my legs. *Wow, that shoulder stiffness has diminished as well,* I noted as my attention scanned back upwards. *The throat tension that has been there for a couple years is there still though. Interesting that I cannot feel any sensation on the front of my neck, but I can feel it in my upper throat.* I tuned in as the next wave of emotion hit me—pure, raw, visceral anger. I felt my fists clench, my posture straighten, and my throat tense even more. *Screw him for not talking to me though. Screw all of them for not trying harder. Why is it always my responsibility?* Heat rose from my stomach and flushed my face and neck, as I allowed it all to come forward. *Why am I always in the wrong? I am accused of over-touching people in public but I cannot even do it in balance in my own life.* My anger turned on myself as my instinct to get up and scream obscenities at the world and stomp out of the room increased. A familiar pain shot through the back of my head. *D*** these headaches! They have been haunting me for years. Enough already!! No matter what I do, it's not enough. It's always wrong.* Shame mingled with the anger, and I gave up as a wave of angry tears burst into a sob.

I stood up and walked out the door and to the woods, where we were allowed to walk silently, although not during meditation time. *Screw everybody. I just don't care. I'll just hide myself behind some trees so no one can find me.*

A few minutes passed, and the emotions subsided. I brought myself back to the forest, to the log I had found to sit on, back to the trail. I listened to the sound of the birds and the wind in the trees, and just sat, feeling completely empty and peaceful.

When I was ready, I stood up and returned silently to the meditation hall. I continued scanning for the next hour, feeling the peace and the softness that had settled over my body. *My throat tension is gone, as is my hip pain. I'm naturally breathing softer. At least my headache subsided, too.* I knew we often carry emotions in our body as physical pain, but I had no clue how insidious mine was.

Pausing to Enjoy the Landscape and Breathe

I had no idea that after that retreat, my headaches would almost permanently subside, my adrenals would come back to balance, and some of the pain I had in my shoulders that I attributed to my work would also disappear.

I shook my head at the body's always-amazing power to heal itself as I sat in silence next to Alan. The game finished, we had been sitting quietly for a few minutes, just being present, while listening to the birds and the wind in the trees.

He broke the silence first. "Well," he said, looking at me with the same compassion he'd shared with me when I was crying the day we first met, "it's time to go."

I smiled sadly at him. "I am so excited for your journey, Alan, and I'm sure we'll keep in touch."

When I get back from Europe, he will be gone volunteering abroad. I may actually never see him again. I was already tuned into myself because of the game, and I could feel simple sadness in my chest, as well as a profound sense of peace throughout the rest of me.

He paused in his usual way as he watched me. "You go to Europe in just a few days. I'm wishing you really safe travels." He stood up from the bench. "Can we get a picture? We don't actually have one."

I smiled and jumped up, glad for the distraction. "Of course. With your phone or mine?"

"We can use mine." He pulled his out of his backpack and then I snuggled in and put my arm around his waist as he put his arm around my shoulders. We smiled as he took a couple pictures. As he checked to make sure they turned out, I grabbed my water bottle and took a couple deep breaths as I felt the emotions bubble up.

"Enjoy your hiking this weekend, and I'm super excited to hear about your experiences in the other countries and cultures," I said as we walked to the parking lot and I kept myself distracted from my emotional state.

I really don't want to start crying. I'm comfortable crying in front of him, but I have to drive the motorcycle. I'll process this when I get home, I promised myself.

"Yeah," he paused, "it will be good to get away after all of the chaos of the last week. I really need to process and be in a still place." He opened his arms, and we gave each other a long, intentional hug, swaying a bit and giving well-wishes for the future.

"Okay, take care," I said, holding back tears and putting on my helmet.

"You too." He stepped back as I started my motorcycle then turned toward his car.

As I pulled onto the street, gratitude filled me. *I am so thankful I was partnered with him at that class. I have learned so much about what I actually want with regard to touch in all of my relationships. I know there will be challenges, and a lot more I am going to need to learn; but I am not going to accept anything less than someone who at least tries to communicate and interact the way he did. I know I can continue creating this with my nephews, my parents, and my friends.*

Winding through the streets, I thought about how I could start using baby steps with my nephews and modeling healthy touch even more in my actions and words before leaving.

Connections would be so much more respectful and fulfilling if we would all take responsibility for our own touch boundaries.

With that in mind, I headed back into the city toward home to put away my motorcycle for the year and start packing.

Remedies
Forest Fires Allow New Growth

Curiosity
It is so important to be aware, curious, and playful with your sensations, emotions, and reactions while consciously deciding how you want to communicate, give, and receive touch with each individual and community. Analyzing my touch sensitivity with Lance and Sofia, as well as with my parents, allowed me to make choices that suited me, rather than approaching these relationships with frustration or avoidance. As you will see in chapter five, curiosity also served me well when I entered different situations and cultures in my next series of adventures. When you find yourself reacting with any sort of intensity, I invite you to get curious not only with yourself, but around others and their actions. It's another skill to hone and grow that can take time but will serve you well in the long run.

Compassion

Compassion is incredibly powerful. I have had many moments when complete strangers have shown me compassion, and they have been some of my most amazing experiences. Alan's gaze during our exercise in class as I experienced the pain of being disconnected is one example of this compassion from a perfect stranger. When I was in Ireland and was very upset in an airport, a woman came up to me, looked at me, and asked if I was okay. I told her I was just very sad, and she touched me on my shoulder and asked if she could do anything. I told her "no," but that reach-out was powerful for me and helped me reset my emotional state. Because of how these acts of compassion have changed my life, I try to offer it to strangers as well. For example, when I see moms trying to soothe their suddenly-upset child, I smile at them and say something kind about the baby. I also listen compassionately while my clients and friends share the life issues they are working through and try to encourage them.

There is another level of compassion though, and it seems to come the hardest for most people, but it is a key to healing: self-compassion. Why is it so hard? Perhaps we are taught that self-compassion is the same as being self-indulgent, that others are supposed to care for us, or that we are not supposed to come first. As you expand your touch and experience the friction of contrary belief systems within your self, or between self and others, be intentional about having compassion for them and their experiences; and please be compassionate toward yourself—your experiences, reactions, sensitivities, and faults—because you must allow room for mistakes and fears to arise. Allowing emotions to arise so you can look at them clearly and with compassion is instrumental in letting them go. As you saw in my meditation experience, sometimes you don't even have to look at them. You can choose neutrality, observe your experience, know it will change and, as the moment shifts, allow it to move through you. Observing the release and having compassion for the part of yourself that is in pain can be one of the greatest gifts you give yourself. Chances are, you would be compassionate for a friend in that kind of pain, so be committed to offering the same experience to yourself.

Communication

Touch communication has many important aspects. In the past few chapters, we have explored internal needs, safety, and consent. Here, we are going to start looking for ways to bring curiosity, communication, compassion, and commitment to your interactions.

You saw how being curious yet also taking charge of my own level of communication in various interactions with Alan allowed not only for a sense of comfort, but it created honesty and openness in our friendship. You also saw, in contrast, how my lack of clear communication in my workspace resulted in a year of pain and isolation in a community that was all about connection and acceptance. If they had known I was feeling rejected, ignored, or left out, I am sure someone would have helped bridge that connection. However, I was not ready to be vulnerable enough to speak with others about what I was feeling. Some of that was my lack of clarity that the isolated feeling was stemming from the lack of touch connection. Unconsciously, I observed all of those touches between others; registered that very few, if any, involved me; and felt each moment of exclusion like a small cut. Of course, just like some of my past relationships, I justified my sense of dis-ease instead of communicating it. I thought I was not connected because I was in my massage room instead of the common areas, I only worked one or two days a week, I was too new to the team, and the list continues. But after two years of the justifications and thinking it would get better on its own, I just gave up. The cuts had become thick scars, and I didn't have the energy or fortitude to resolve the situation. I didn't want to make anyone feel bad that I had felt excluded for so long. I didn't want to admit, even to myself, that it was my fault that I was isolated, and that this group relationship was not working for me anymore.

This experience awakened a realization that I equate physical contact with connection. In chapter one, I asked you to look at what you equate touch with in different areas of your life. Past experiences with physical contact may have been hurtful, isolating, shaming, or anger-inducing. It may have been a tool for manipulation, control, or punishment. If this is the case for you, it may be hard for you to believe the research that shows how our neurons and chemical reactions encourage trust, collaboration, and generosity when we engage in touch—how it fosters a feeling of connection, being nurtured, and belonging. That's why it is important that we do this work to heal from our wounds, forgive others and ourselves for the past, and learn to ask for physical contact with clarity of choice for self and others. When we do this, we can change so much. We can heal our families, communities, and the world we live in.

Commitment

When I look back at how much easier it was for me to manage the pain of letting go of old relationships that had *not* created great levels of pain inside (the one with Alan) versus letting go of one that created months of disturbances and pain (the one with James), the importance of committing to release old emotions becomes even more clear. Humans have a great capacity for carrying pain, anger, and emotional baggage from place to place, and relationship to relationship, without realizing it. When we do not have an experience of healthy give-and-take in our lives, it can show up as physical, mental, or emotional stress, pain, and disease. When we do not have clarity on what is happening, why it is happening, or what we feel about it, the same triggers will keep showing up in different ways. Like that friend who keeps dating the type of person who is bad for them. Or the person who, just as financial success is within reach, has a tragedy that causes financial strain or ruin. Or the individual who starts exercising to get healthy and, as soon as they are in the groove, becomes injured.

When I told people I was writing a book to help people bring healthy and consensual touch into their lives and communities, I experienced two reactions. 1. Wow, we really need that and I can't wait to read it. 2. That's a taboo/challenging subject, so good luck. This is a SENSITIVE TOPIC because bad things have happened and continue to happen. The cultural changes in abuse awareness, touch in the workplace, empowerment of women, role and power dynamics, and the opening of communication around both sexual and non-sexual touch has left many of us empowered to speak out about transgressions but also terrified to have any form of physical contact with anyone beyond family and close friends.

For example, how many of you had a hard time believing that Alan and I could experience so much non-sexual touch and enjoy it without any of the normal stress we associate intimate touch with in our culture? Intimacy can be intellectual, emotional, experiential, spiritual, or physical; but just because it is physical does not mean it is sexual.

The "me too" movement, founded in 2006 by Tarana Burke to support survivors of sexual violence, particularly women of color, exploded when the hashtag #MeToo became viral and highlighted the extent of sexual violence worldwide.[55] The expansion of "me too" has been important for so many people to finally speak up and be heard. I know women who have had to have sex with their boss to keep their job and women who were groped inappropriately at work, in public, and at parties. Women (and men) have been sexually assaulted and raped at a variety of ages, and I had some of my own close-calls when I was younger. I am not discounting or downplaying any of these experiences. I understand many of these people could not say *no*, or they said *no* and their *no* was not heard. Or they were told their *no* was wrong. Or their *no* was manipulated so the other could feel empowered by denying that *no*. I also understand that many survivors cannot access the specific details as they speak out about what happened to them, which is a blessing and part of the body's protective mechanism. However, this whole conversation can inspire us to think about what we are feeling when we think about unwanted touch.

- Are we feeling immediately violated because the touch is blatant, yet we play it off as something unimportant? Are we not speaking up because we feel we cannot not speak up or will not be heard?

- Is it possible that some of us perhaps do not feel violated until later, when someone tells us we should feel that way about a touch we received long ago because we have had no clarity for ourselves on what touch is inappropriate, healthy, or consensual.

- Is there a path to healing we can take as individuals and a culture by acknowledging the situation and using it as a learning tool for the future?

For example, my butt has been grabbed and people have placed a hand on me without consent a bunch of times. Many of these times, I was not offended or upset in that moment, perhaps because I did not understand my boundaries, or maybe even because I saw it as a compliment or as attention. Sometimes the interaction felt playful and I focused on the intent of the touch rather than the location of touch. But I can use those memories to form how I want to react to future situations in a way that feels empowering to me, and perhaps even gentle to the other.

When I question the reactions of some of the people who are speaking up, I am *not* saying what happened was right or their memories are invalid because they cannot remember certain details.

What I *am* saying is that our memories are malleable, and perhaps sometimes we make assumptions that are untrue or get stuck on the incident rather than looking for a path to understanding, self-power, and healing. For example, I read an article by a woman who described having to give hugs to her male abuser at the end of family events because he was part of the family, and it was part of the satisfaction he got, as well as one of the ways he kept her silent. For her, the sick sneer on his face is one that consistently confirmed that he was abusive and he knew it. However, I also read another article where a woman described her violation by a male in college. He recognized himself in the description and contacted her, contrite and apologetic. He told her he had no idea he had made her feel that way or had pushed her too far. This response indicates a lack of clarity and communication around touch in the relationship or the culture in which the interactions are taking place.

Regardless of whether the touch was intentionally abusive, the result of not being internally clear or communicating clearly around what was acceptable or not, these women both felt violated and had some healing work to do around the violations.

If you have had similar experiences, it is important to commit to your healing. We cannot change how we felt back then; but we can do work to release and neutralize emotions (not stuff them or ignore them) so we can look back with little to no trigger and, more importantly, move into a phase of enjoying and benefiting from healthy touch. You cannot always choose what happens to you, but you can always choose how you respond.

Moving forward, we have to commit to creating safety for ourselves and others with touch in all situations. We are taught to endure touch a lot when we are young. We do not have the right to say how people wipe our butt and change our diapers and when we get held and when we don't as infants. We can cry and wiggle and show our displeasure, but if there is a diaper catastrophe, there really is not time for the adult to wait until baby is willing to get clean. Some of us were made to give hugs to people who did not feel safe to us. Many of us were placed in unsafe situations by people we trusted. Some of us are still in unsafe situations, even as adults. Perhaps we are observing a potentially unsafe situation and do not want to get involved. Maybe our reptilian brain is telling us something is unsafe when it may not be.

Take a deep breath, commit to making a change for the better, and tap into any resource you can find to assist you, no matter how difficult it seems and how many obstacles your brain tries to put into your way.

How do we make true progress in healing our ability to accept, give, and appreciate physical contact? We start with committing to curiosity, communication, and compassion despite all of the emotional turbulence we may have to experience to heal the past. We will make the most progress if we have compassion for ourselves and others, commit to communicating clearly internally and externally and make generous assumptions that people are probably doing the best they can in every moment.

Touch Trails and Connections:

One chaplain I interviewed had once sat holding a dying man's hand while talking to his grandchild. The child asked, "What do you do?" The chaplain replied, "This is my medicine."

Another woman I interviewed works with newborn babies. She commented that she likes to hold the babies facing outward so they have a feeling that "I've got their back."

One man I interviewed spoke about a hospital stay he experienced. He would ask the nurses to tell him something that made them happy that day. The touch he received from the nurses who played along felt more connected and nurturing than those who tended him in a rush or who wouldn't answer.

One study trained ten teachers in classroom management, then evaluated a control group (teachers that made no effort to greet students at the beginning of the day) to a positive greeting group (teachers that greeted their students in a positive manner at the door.) "For the control group, little changed. Time on task was in the mid-to-high 50%, while disruptive behaviors took place about 15% of the time. For the positive greeting group, researchers saw big changes. Time on task went from the high-50% to more than 80% of the time. Disruptive behaviors fell from ~15% to less than 5% of the time."[56]

One study showed the physical impact of touch-based support in partnerships. "Greater partner support (based on self-report) was related to higher plasma oxytocin in men and women before and after warm contact. In women, higher partner support was correlated with lower systolic blood pressure during solitary rest after warm contact but not before. Also, higher oxytocin in women was linked to lower blood pressure at baseline and to lower norepinephrine..."[57]

"Across a number of studies, researchers have found that touching the person you are asking for a favour significantly increases the chance of them agreeing to your request. As the favour asked becomes larger, touch plays a more important role. This is particularly so when you are asking help from someone of the same gender."[58]

The same type of touch can be interpreted in different ways, depending on the receiver's mental state. "Touching another person isn't just a one-way street when it comes to signaling; aside from sending them a message, it reveals a great of deal of information about their state of mind. Are they open to touch or do they pull away? Are they relaxed or tense? Are they warm— or perhaps cold and clammy?" Think about it this way. A gentle caress on the arm from a partner while you are having fun is received much differently than a gentle caress when you are in the middle of an argument.[59]

"The true indicator of a healthy long-term bond is not how often your partner touches you but how often he or she touches you in *response* to your touch."[60]

> Consider reaching out to touch those who have lost a long-term partner. As one woman put it, losing a long-term partner can be like your favorite chef-owned restaurant burning down. At first, everyone gives condolences to the owner; but after a while, they find a new place to eat. Yet the owner is left behind, sitting alone in the ashes of what used to be their life.

Delving into the 4 C's

Communication
I understand that real-life communities and relationships do not always function so well. There are power differentials, technical failures, projects and people needing attention, financial plans going astray, and miscommunications over words said and unsaid. However, what I do see clearly is the opportunity to understand our own wants around touch, and to learn to vocalize clearly and with strong intention. Your *no* to a hug, a volunteer position, or a project you do not have time for comes from the same space of knowing your want. The key is having the tools, the words, and the confidence to state it clearly.

As you move through various levels and stages of integrating touch into your life, remember you can also make a powerful connection by just simply letting people know that you are honoring them and yourself by requesting touch as well as declining touch. We each get to release the internal dialogues of what, or why, or whom, or what is appropriate or not appropriate, or why is that person not doing "X" or why am I not doing "Y." When those stories and beliefs are released and you can become present in the moment with yourself and the other person, you are creating value and connection that is both honorable and lasting.

Yet, many of us feel guilt, doubt, or fear when we say *no* to something or someone. Choosing your words to show you are saying *no* to an action but *yes* to the person is extremely powerful. Think about all the ways we can do this for the people we love through the following examples:

- "You are a good friend, and you don't get to speak to me that way."
- "I appreciate your viewpoint, and please show respect for others when you comment on my posts."
- "I have fun playing ball with you, and it hurts when you head-butt me."
- "I know you are exhausted, and please don't use that tone with me."
- "I would love to hug you right now, and may I please put away the groceries first?"
- "My drive home was really stressful and I need a few minutes to calm down. Can we talk in five?"

- "I know you want to explain right now, and I am too angry to hear you clearly."
- "Thank you for buying me a coffee, and I am sorry that before I can listen to the rest of your story I have to reply to my boss. Can you give me three minutes and then you will have my undivided attention?"
- "I love that you are rubbing my shoulder, and it is starting to tickle. Can you move to my neck/use a harder pressure/stop for now?"

These are examples of phrases that make an attempt to acknowledge the other person's needs as well as our own. *Yes* to the person, *no* to the action.

It's also important to note that we do not have to say *yes* to the person unless we choose to. We can communicate our wants and needs clearly, and if someone asks us to expand we can choose to do so in order to create safety, understanding, connection, or whatever is needed to facilitate the conversation. Just be clear that when we are opening conversation, our "why" is not up for negotiation—it is a feeling, emotion, or something that the other cannot dispute. Most of us have learned when we say *no*, we must defend ourselves—with excuses, justifications, or explanations—usually in an attempt to prove to the other we are serious or to avoid the feeling of conflict or rejection. For example, I see people defend their *no* in many ways.

"No, I can't…

- drink because I have to drive home."
- eat dessert because am trying to lose weight."
- talk because I am too tired."
- do that project because I told my kids I would spend more time with them."

Yes these are all valid, but there are a number of valid reasons why we would choose to say *no* to something without needing to defend ourselves. We can learn to say *no* or *No, thank you* or play with language such as *I'm not interested*. We do not have to put off or avoid saying *no*. We may think defending our decision makes it stronger, but it weakens it. We do not owe anyone an explanation. Instead, we can remember how we feel when we really want to do something and say *yes* strongly. Then we can use the same power with our *no*. I remember a teacher at a workshop saying, "When you have a strong and clear *no*, it also communicates to others that when you say *yes*, you mean it. This makes both your *no* and your *yes* stronger."

This concept can be applied universally, especially around touch. By practicing saying *no* with someone safe, when we run into a time or situation when we are "all-touched-out" or uncomfortable, we can clearly state what we need.

If we approach our communication with others this way, when someone says *no* to us, instead of taking it personally, we can easily accept it as the other person speaking what they need in the moment rather than as a rejection of us. As Don Miguel Ruiz, Jr. says in his book *The Four Agreements*, "Don't take anything personally. What others do is not about you."[61]

For example, my friend Jon shared an exercise he experienced at a cuddle party. (Yes, those really exist.) The purpose of the exercise was to practice saying *no* without feeling like you were rejecting the other person, while the other person practiced not feeling rejected. The exchange went something as follows:

Person 1: "May I hug you?"
Person 2: "No."
Person 1: "Thank you for taking care of yourself."
Person 2: "May I rub your shoulder?"
Person 1: "No."
Person 2: "Thank you for taking care of yourself."

After practicing this, Jon says that he doesn't take *no* personally anymore. He does not have a sense of rejection because he has reframed his brain into knowing that the other person, without having to give a justification or a reason, is just taking care of his/her own needs at the moment and speaking that truth. Simple, isn't it? Can you speak your needs with such clarity? When someone says *no* to you, will you make the choice to take it with grace—to feel honored that they are speaking honestly and that their *no* has nothing to do with you? We all have a fear of being rejected, so many of us make a choice not to ask at all. When you make that choice, you deny yourself what you want or need, *and* you deny another an opportunity to say *yes* or *no*. If you ask a person for a hug, and that person says *no*, not only have you shown them respect by asking in the first place, but they have shown you respect by not lying to you. That alone can create a sense of respect and safety in any situation.

Intentions
There is a moment in each of our lives where our parents, grandparents, or someone who routinely played a nurturing role in our lives picked us up for the last time or gave us our last cuddle. For some of us it was in infancy, and we cannot draw upon a single memory. For others, it happened as we grew, changed, or became independent. For some it happened because touch was not available, was not safe, or was not acceptable. When I look at my parents or my nephews, I get curious. When is the last time going to be? It makes me remember, when I do have an opportunity to hug my mom or feel my nephew snuggle in tight so we can read a book, that I want the quality of my touch and my interactions to be present and focused. I want to transmit the care and affection and respect I feel for each of them. Someday, I will have to tell my nephew, "I would love to pick you up, but you're getting so big. How about we just sit together on the couch?" I will have to say *no* to his action of picking up his cell phone and ignoring me while we are together, while saying *yes* to his needs and him as an individual. I want to prepare now so when the time comes, my words will be clear and honest.

My good friend, Liza, is very clear with her touch and will immediately redirect someone if she is feeling uncomfortable in any way. (She practices this in many areas of her life, not just touch.) Everyone she hugs, she hugs with intention, love, and awareness—no matter their relationship to her. I have never felt anything less from her, and I hear others make similar comments. I remember a time with my friend Dave, whom she had just met that evening, but had shared he had been going through some depression. We were all giving goodbye hugs, and Dave went to give Liza a quick hug goodbye. As he pulled back, she said, "Nope, just feel it." He settled back in, took a breath, and I saw him physically relax and soften. Even when Liza is in need of consolation, she is completely present and aware and loving, even though she is receiving rather than giving. If we strive for a higher level of communication and intention when we touch each other, I bet all of our relationships would be a lot different.

What's your favorite touch moment? Ursula Mentjes, Entrepreneur and Sales Coach, shared hers with me: "I was in a group coaching program, and our coach gave the best hugs. We would all even joke about it. I can't even explain. The way she wrapped her arms around each of us was such a well-meaning hug, as if it was the healing we needed. When she hugged you, it was a longer hug and there was an intention; it felt as if she was thinking a positive thought or blessing. The whole energy felt as if she was infusing goodness and hope and possibility into that hug. She hugged every one of us like that. Because of that hug, I felt included. I can still feel exactly what that felt like. It made me a better and more intentional hugger."

Imagine for a moment, after you ask someone if they would like a hug, and you receive a *yes*, setting the intention for that hug to transmit as much goodness and love as possible through you, while also opening yourself to receive that back. Really, close your eyes for a moment and feel how that would feel in your body. When you are able to feel and/or give even a bit of that kind of connection, pure magic can happen for you and the community around you.

I invite you to practice setting an intention before giving a consensual hug or putting your hand on someone's shoulder—to really transmit that energy you want to share with that person through the touch.

Extra Support for the Healing Journey

Having a non-judgmental support system and tools that work for you to help you process your own triggers is essential. For example, the personal tools I use include EFT/tapping, forgiveness and gratitude walks, Bach flower essences, body dialoguing, journaling, and a variety of different meditations. My professional support system includes my homeopath, bodyworkers, mentors, and other EFT practitioners. Your support system and tools will help create a mindful space where you can prevent yourself from getting yanked into old patterns and even release them as they arise.

Consider your own forms of daily self-care. What if part of the reason we do not like to touch is because we are so busy in our daily lives giving our energy to our work, our partners, our kids, and our friends, that we are not taking anything—including enjoyment, comfort, or rejuvenation from touch—while we are emptying our buckets? No wonder we avoid touch. Add the emotional baggage and the societal fears and suddenly, like a stay-at-home mom of two toddlers, we do not have a spare moment where we are able to nurture ourselves with the touch we give or receive.

An Internal Peek

Do you take it personally when others say no to you? Why do you think that is? How might you say yes to a person and no to touch with someone in your life?

Think of one or two ways you can intentionally nurture yourself using touch. What is the easiest way to add this into your daily routine?

I invite you to turn to the "Play & Explore" section and do exercises one and two under communication in chapter four in the back of the book for a more thorough exploration.

Once that is complete, exercise four is the final column from exercise three in chapter three. Explore a timeline that feels powerful for you.

"Too often we underestimate the power of a touch, a smile, a kind word, a listening ear, an honest compliment, or the smallest act of caring, all of which have the potential to turn a life around."

~ Leo Buscaglia, American author and motivational speaker ~

CHAPTER 5
CAMPFIRES & COOKOUTS
Comparing Landscapes and Sharing the Adventure

Navigating Communal Touch Terrain

The Island of Senja is such a beautiful place, I thought, as I drove my friend's car around the point and followed the curve of the northern-Norwegian fjord back away from the sea. I had spent all day hiking alone and was on my way to a beach area known for having a great space for wild (free) camping yet also water access, portable toilets, and a beach. *I usually prefer wild camping away from people and drinking water from the mountains, but I've been isolated too long. It will be nice to be around people and have some real conversations.* According to websites, many people stayed there and it was quite busy. *I even have wine with me to share.*

The friend I was visiting had shared a lot of the nuances of Norwegian culture: "They need a logical reason to have a conversation with someone. You don't just go meet someone for coffee to get to know them, and you do not say 'hi' casually on the streets or in public. They will talk a lot if they are drinking a lot, but then they may not talk to you the next day." Not only had she told me what to expect, she had shared a book that was written on the subject, complete with funny stick-figure drawings that confirmed her observations over the last fifteen years. *She did say people would say hello on the trails, but I didn't experience any of that today unless someone was asking a question about direction or timing.*

I arrived and found a parking space. The beach was nestled inside a small fjord overlooking the Norwegian Sea. The narrow, barely two-lane road split the camping area, with the white sand beach on my right and a long meadow on the left, before rising steeply into cliffs that formed the other three sides. *The sun is in a perfect spot right now. It's coming directly over the water to keep the area warm, but will disappear around that mountain so it's hidden through most of the night. Midnight sun is beautiful and amazing, but not when it's heating my tent all night long.* I paused for a minute, feeling some of the unusual tension in my body. *Between the lack of touch and all-night sun, my hormones are really confused.* It was only 5 p.m., but there were already around a hundred RV/campers and an equal amount of tents spread throughout the area. *I can't believe I left my swimsuit at home. I did not expect it to be this warm today.* I eyed the adults and children playing in the sea with envy. *I don't know if my clothes would dry overnight if I swam in them, and twenty miles of mountain hiking would be unbearable with wet shorts.*

I grabbed my rucksack from the car and headed to the meadow. *I also don't need sand in everything I own.* The meadow had a series of long grasses and knolls alternating with flat areas, most of which had some sort of firepit. I set up my tent in a flat area, close to three other tents but far enough away that we would all have privacy. I greeted the brown-haired, fifty-something woman sitting in her low camping chair at the tent closest to me, who looked up from her book as I walked by. She nodded and looked back down quickly. *Hmm. Well, she is into her book. Or maybe she is from another country and assumes I'm Norwegian and doesn't feel like speaking another language.* I had noticed there were equal parts Norske and foreigners on the trails, although all had seemed to adopt the "no speaking" rule.

After walking in the water for a while on the beach to cool off, I headed back to my tent to cook dinner on my camping stove. I positioned myself to face the other tents, which seemed empty except for the woman with the book and a man who had joined her. *Even if they had any kind of open body language, they'd be a bit far away to talk to without yelling. And I have a sense they won't welcome me enthusiastically if I just pop over to chat.* I made my rice, lentils, and sausages in a one-pot format, and poured myself a glass of wine.

As I watched I saw people interacting in their immediate circles but not with those neighboring them. *Bummer! People are not interacting, even though they are next to each other with no barriers.* I finished my meal and stood to go to the toilets, where there was an outside tap for showering and washing dishes.

I walked by a series of tents, continuing to observe the quiet way in which people were talking around their drinks and meals. Arriving, I surveyed the scene. *There is no one talking here either. Huh.* I felt confused and a bit uncomfortable at the realization that people were in their own orderly bubbles, almost as if the people around them did not exist. *It feels like a sci-fi alternate universe movie. A whole line for the toilets, a separate line for the showers and tap, and a group of people hanging around; and no one is interacting beyond a soft meeting of the eyes here and there before they look elsewhere again.* I watched a mom speak to her kids under the shower as she encouraged them to hurry and get all the sand off of themselves. Another woman stood just beside her, empty water tank in hand, obviously next in line. A couple to my right had a dishpan and were washing their dishes quietly. A three-year-old girl was playing in the water streaming from the concrete into the sand from the shower, alternating between being absorbed in her work and gazing at the people around her while her dad stood protectively and silently nearby. *Not even interactions with the children. In Minnesota, people at least say hello to the children or engage with curiosity if they are looking at them.* Feeling out of place and not willing to push the cultural norm, I got in line compliantly and kept my silence as a gentle wave of disappointment washed from my head to my toes. *So much for interacting with others and having conversations. It feels like I'd be the "obnoxious American" if I started trying to engage, and I don't want to be that. I wish there was an easy "in" somewhere. I can't even think of a question that would be practical that I could ask someone to try to start conversation.*

After washing up I returned to my campsite, where two guys were sitting on the log next to the cold fire pit near my tent. They looked like hikers in their late twenties, and sat side-by-side facing the sea, talking quietly to each other. *I can't even tell what language they are speaking. I wonder...* I watched them as I walked by, half-smile on my face, ready to engage if either looked up. *Nope. Not even a glance up as I walked past. Geesh.*

I read my kindle near my tent and kept my eyes open for opportunities to engage, but none presented themselves. After popping into my car for my online meeting, I returned to my tent to sleep, observing the people as I passed. *Eleven-thirty p.m. If anyone is drinking heavily, there is no clue. No sudden bursts of laughter, no sudden voice carrying over the area— nothing. Even the kids playing around the fires aren't making much noise.* I could feel the heaviness in my stomach as I puzzled through this situation. Having my social needs unmet, while also adapting to the surreal feeling of the space, created restlessness in my body. *It's like I don't belong here in a major way. Like I should pack up and find a different place to sleep. I'd rather be by myself in the wild than surrounded by people and still feel isolated.* Realizing I was in a perfect spot for sleeping and I had no idea where the next opportunity to camp would present itself, I settled into my tent without even bothering to grab my earplugs.

Man! This is A LOT different than the last time I was in Europe. It was so much easier to engage with those cultures. I really miss interacting with people who are interested in learning about each other. Immersing oneself in a different space of any kind takes such a level of awareness and respect. Some situations just feel so much easier than others.

Witnessing Cultural Landscapes

I dropped my rucksack on the floor next to the only empty lower bunk in the small hostel room and sat down on the bed to strip off my hiking boots, properly wet from the Scottish rain.

"I cannot tell you how glad we are to have you here," gushed the twenty-something woman lying on the bunk opposite mine. "We have been so short on help. I've been here all summer, and we usually have six people around. Now we only have three." She threw her long, dark hair over her shoulder as she sat up, pulling her earbuds out of her ears and setting them on the phone next to her.

"It's good to be here, and it helps me, too."

Heck, I'll volunteer a couple hours a day to meet people and learn new things while I'm traveling. Sharing a room with staff is a bonus, as I don't have to worry about theft.

"You're American," she stated, picking up on my accent quickly. "What part? I'm Lexi, by the way. I'm from Mexico, going to uni in England, and working here in Scotland over the summer."

"Minnesota," I answered, pulling my clothes out of my rucksack so I could shove my camping gear under the bed for the duration of my stay.

"Oh my gosh! I love American football and I really love the Vikings. They are my favorite team behind the Broncos." She got up and grabbed my arm, her curvy frame moving quickly across the room. "Come on, let me show you around and introduce you to everyone. I think they're all in the kitchen drinking tea."

Still gently holding onto my arm, she led me through an open door into a bright cozy kitchen space with a countertop bar separating it from the small dining room, where there were about eight people scattered around a few tables, talking cheerily over steaming mugs.

"Hey everybody! This is Dawn!" Lexi exclaimed loudly in a proper British accent, arm now comfortably on my shoulder like we had been friends forever. "She's from Minnesota, where the Vikings are from." She gave me a firm squeeze and then introduced me to the guests and staff in the room. "This is Katrin," she said, giving a fifty-something German woman a squeeze from behind. "She's here writing a book. This is Frenchie," she continued, saying a few words in French and giving the tall, thin guy in line a peck on the cheek. "We've been working together for a month or so by now. This is Juan—he's from Spain," she continued, putting her hand enthusiastically on the shoulder of a dark-haired middle-aged man. "He's staying here only tonight with his friends."

I already like her, especially the way she is so connected with touching everyone. I know it's part of her culture, but it flows so smoothly and is so genuine. I wonder if she's ever had anyone get offended.

"Grab coffee or tea, Dawn. It's free for staff and guests. Hang out. Chat. We'll do the tour later," Lexi continued, flopping into a chair as she asked some newcomers where they were from and how long they'd be around.

I grabbed some instant coffee and settled into the space, watching Lexi continue her casual contact with the majority of people.

She's very good at inclusion. It's not only about the way she touches. I can see people relaxing as she engages them in conversation and introduces them to others. I heard her say a few words in what I thought was Italian and shook my head, completely impressed. *She seems to have mastered the skill of bridging cultural gaps, at least at a first-world-country level.*

The kitchen area remained the center of activity for the weeks I was there, and it became quite the cultural learning opportunity for me.

On my third day there was heavy rain in the evening, creating a particularly busy and chaotic scene. People had flooded into the hostel around the same time and were busily cooking and eating.

I was chopping some veggies at the counter for my salad when I felt a hand on the side of my right calf, as a woman from Australia alerted me of her presence before grabbing some plates from the lower cupboard. A few minutes later, the woman from India I'd met before came up behind me on the left, and allowed part of her short, athletic frame to contact mine as she reached in front of me to the upper cupboard to grab a couple of glasses. "Hello," she said smiling.

"Busy kitchen. Sorry if I'm in your way." I offered, ducking a bit to try to give her a better angle.

She laughed brightly. "Ah, it's worse in India. I swear, we have no personal boundaries sometimes. No apologies—we are always bumping into others in the market and on the bus. It's just expected that you will get brushed against."

"I want to go sometime. So is touch really no big deal there?" I asked, suddenly curious.

"If you have a reasonably good working relationship or know someone and you touch them, they understand you are getting their attention or looking for more of a bond. It's just how we are in general. It varies a bit from area to area. India is pretty big, you know." She laughed again, dark eyes sparkling, and glided away.

It's so interesting how the people who come from cultures where touch is normal have little to no personal space, whereas the cultures who have bigger personal bubbles are more evident in this kind of crowd. As if to reaffirm my observation, an Asian woman appeared to my right, and asked if she could please get into the same cupboard to grab a glass. I moved aside, observing as she retrieved what she needed, and managed to make her way smoothly back to her table without touching anyone in the bustling kitchen. *Part is politeness, but hers is not a touch-forward culture.* As I washed and dried the cutting board and knife, I had at least three more people touch me to either warn me of their presence or to nudge me a bit so they could access what they needed.

"Can I join you all?" I directed my question randomly to some people on the bench that ran the full length of the wall. They skootched together as much as possible, and I squeezed through the haphazard layout of tables and chairs to claim my inches of space between two strangers. *Personal space and touch boundaries are a work in process here. I suppose if people don't like touch, they would naturally avoid this situation.* I watched to see how the Asians were interacting. *They don't seem to mind being crowded, but they aren't casually touching others or reaching across the table to grab things.* It was a stark contrast to the four rowdy Irish next to them, who reached across each other for condiments and food. *The women from China I met in Stockholm were okay with hugs and touch with me though.* A different realization hit and my stomach dropped a bit in angst. *Or maybe they were tolerating it because I was so enthusiastic and willing to engage them, kind of like Lexi, or because they were being polite. On the other hand, perhaps they were choosing to be culturally open and welcomed the experience. Speaking of which...*

I focused on the people around me and joined the conversation.

The Next Cookout

I quietly climbed out of my tent the next morning when the midnight sun was peeking around the other side of the mountain. As I cooked breakfast in silence, I thought again longingly of that Scotland hostel. *Those interactions were not only life-changing, but I really enjoyed being in a space where I could get an experience of so many cultures at once. I bet if I make an effort, I can use a blend of respect for this culture and my own personality and awareness to create opportunities for connection, communication, and perhaps even touch here, too.* The next place I was planning to camp was a ferry-crossing town, and I figured there would be a more diverse blend of cultures there. Feeling excited again, I hurriedly took down my campsite and headed out for another day of hiking and possibility.

I drove the small car through the Norwegian fjord into the town of Gryllefjord, looking for a place to wild camp. Feeling strong and resolved in my core to have a different experience, I turned my attention to the small signs advertising local events and restaurants.

Whoa! Was that a sign saying free camping and toilet! I slowed down and found the next place to turn around. *SCORE!* I had already rinsed off in a fresh water stream after my strenuous five hours of hiking, expecting to be wild camping in a meadow somewhere for the evening. *I wanted to stay close enough to walk into town, and I have an actual free campground!*

I drove into the well-manicured entrance with a small gazebo and pond. There were a series of gravel roads heading into the forest that reminded me of the camping areas at Minnesota State Parks, with signs indicating designated camping spots. *It's empty right now,* I marveled as I drove around. *There are only six or so camping spots, but I would expect people to be all over this space, especially because of the real toilet.* I pulled over, getting out of my car to look at the secluded spaces up each path. *I can smell both the forest and the*

Norwegian sea here. Oh, and I and see the fjord through the trees from the picnic table at this one. I quickly set up camp, anxious to interact with people. *Only a twenty-minute walk to town along the road that parallels the fjord.*

With a spring in my step, I set off to the simple restaurant I had chosen. My dad had offered to buy me my birthday dinner, and I was looking forward to sitting outside and looking over the water while eating something traditional from the menu. *And hopefully some good chats.* A series of small RVs holding tourists from all over Norway and other countries were in line in the old seaside town, waiting for the ferry. *I can't even imagine paying for the fuel over here for one of those things. But, for those who don't want to interact with others, it is the perfect way to travel.* I glanced into the dark windows of the practical shops as I passed. *It adds to the feeling that I will be isolated again tonight unless there are drunk people at the bar.*

The restaurant had the feel of a small, simple café, complete with a tall Norwegian blonde woman behind a coffee counter and a glass case full of baked goods. Wanting to feel part of the culture, I walked up and grabbed the Norwegian menu. *Maybe I can figure this out.* I was a little nervous, as I really wanted to connect, but wasn't sure what was appropriate as far as initiating conversation. *Will I talk to people in English? Swedish/Norwegian hybrid? Well, I don't understand much of this menu, so it's already looking bad.* I traded it for English and skimmed the page. *No wonder. Whale steak, some kind of fish I've never heard of, and accoutrements I barely understand in English.* After ordering, I regathered my courage and sauntered upstairs into the near-empty open dining room that included a small stage to my left and a bar to my right. The windows overlooked the ferry, fjord, and small patio which was packed. Most of the inside chairs had been pulled outside and added to tables crowded with people and drinks. *That's okay. I've been outside all day. It won't hurt me to sit inside near the windows.* After claiming a chair by loading it with my stuff, I sauntered up to the bar for a glass of wine just as the bartender ran to the back. I waited patiently, and a tall, stocky, obviously-Norwegian gentleman and a shorter brunette woman joined me in the wait.

"Var är han?" the man asked, followed by something I didn't understand, as he gestured toward the back and then down the stairs I had ascended earlier.

"Du talar för fort. Jag föstar inte. Kan du säga det igen?" I said, telling him in Swedish that he spoke too fast and I needed him to repeat what he'd said. I focused intently on the general words as he asked if the bartender was in back or getting food from the kitchen.

"Is English easier?" he asked.

I nodded. "Yes, but I should have a conversation to learn."

The woman chimed in and my brain immediately tried to pinpoint her accent, "It's really a friendly space here. You can just pull up at any table and join the conversation. Are you waiting for the ferry as well?"

When the bartender returned and took their order, I paused. *Just pull up and join the conversation?* I felt my stomach flip. *From what I know, that might not be appropriate. Plus with those full tables, it seems like a lot to manage with a plate full of food.*

Dawn, my other voice chided, *you would have jumped on that in three seconds at home, plus that's what you resolved to do. Remember being in Ireland in 2009? You had no compunction about joining conversations, touching people, engaging, and being yourself. Yes, you are more culturally sensitive now, as well as more aware of the impact of unwanted touch on people; but don't hide out at the perfect moment.*

I shook my head at myself. *I'm back to being sensitive to people and a bit fearful of overstepping cultural boundaries. Perhaps I can bridge that with more ease this time—after I eat at a proper table.*

"Miss, what can I get you?" the bartender asked.

When we all had our drinks, we started introductions. The woman was German and was traveling Norway in an RV with her husband and three large dogs. The man was from Oslo, Norway, and was on a two-week holiday visiting friends. Both returned to their respective groups on the patio. My food arrived and I was grateful for the space while people-watching through the glass. *People are sitting very close to each other, and most are laughing, engaging, and talking with enthusiasm, but they are not touching casually at all. Even the couples don't seem to be touching much.*

"Come, join us outside." The German lady peeked her head in the door, her shoulder-length curly hair standing out from under her beanie. "Don't be in here all by yourself."

"I was just going to eat first and then come out," I said, startled and hesitant to leave my quiet nest, "but okay."

"How can I help? Shall I grab your water and wine?" she asked, as she reached forward to grab them.

"Thank you." I followed her with my food out to the corner table, where her husband sat.

The couple sharing their table must have left. I didn't even notice.

She set my drinks down and introduced her husband. Quickly, we started with casual talk about our trips, and eventually worked our way into other conversations as we ordered another round of wine.

This is what I've wanted for so many days. A connection with people, real conversation, and a chance to learn.

"You are more than welcome to come stay with us in Germany," she offered, her husband nodding as she pulled out her phone. "We are in a really small town, but it is beautiful. Here, I'll show you."

Everywhere I travel, I meet good, generous people who want to share where they come from and who are proud and excited to share it with others.

We exchanged Facebook messages so I had the ability to contact them in December, the next time I would be able to enter the Schengen zone again.

"Okay, we have to get our dogs out for a while," she said, standing up. "We will see you in Germany."

Okay, this is my opportunity to practice what I preach.

I took a breath and stood, being careful to keep my body open and relaxed. "How do you say goodbye where you come from? Do you just say goodbye and wave? Give handshakes? Hugs? What's appropriate?" I smiled, watching her reaction to my question.

It feels like a way to imply I am open for all of those things, but without crossing a cultural barrier and asking for something specific. Even though we have been talking for two hours, we are technically strangers. I know Germans have a reputation for being practical and structured, but I have no idea how they touch.

"Hugs are good," she replied smiling and opened her arms. We exchanged a warm hug, and I stepped back from the table.

I am not sure how it goes with the husband. I will just wait and see. I turned and smiled at him, but he had already moved toward me, and gave me a quicker, but still very genuine hug.

"Enjoy the rest of your trip," I said with my heart full of happiness, "and I will see you both soon."

After I finished my meal, I walked through the town and reflected on the evening. I'd had a lot of experiences in Europe, and even though I had set a strong intention, I had almost stopped believing it was possible to have such a warm conversation and share hugs with perfect strangers while in Norway.

I'm really grateful and I want to carry this over into my hike tomorrow. It seems there are a lot of people from other areas of Europe visiting this area. I bet if I play with greeting others on the trail, I can get another level of understanding as I observe who engages in return and how they do it. Perhaps this is a small way that I can start really practicing and shifting a cultural experience, even if it is only for myself.

I sat on a bench, watched the sun creep behind the fjord, sent a few messages and pictures home, and then returned to my campsite, grateful for the evening and hopeful for the next day.

A Warm Respite

I slept really well and woke up excited to hike the glacier. Mindful of my determination to engage the night before, I grabbed my toothbrush and camelback water sack and headed toward the bathroom.

"Hello," I said in English to the couple packing up their tent near their car, almost forgetting I was in a foreign country.

"Hi," they both replied and smiled as I walked past.

Success!! I felt my step lighten as my social experiment began in what I considered a positive way. *I don't know what that accent was—perhaps Baltic? Either way, this day is looking up. That oxytocin hit really helped last night.* I smiled to myself, remembering the hugs.

I packed up and headed out for my long drive. When I arrived at the glacial trailhead, I surveyed the busy gravel parking lots and confirmed my bug spray, snacks, and water were all in my backpack.

There must be thirty cars here, plus that small bus. I'm not surprised it's busy, considering the lack of steep peaks and challenging cliffs. The hike was advertised as a four-to-five-hour medium-difficulty journey through a series of valleys. Most of the trail followed the river formed by the glacial runoff. *It will be a busy trail. I know there are another two or three trails here that I will hit afterwards, if I have the energy; but I bet most are like me and are here for the main attraction.*

I turned on tracking on my watch and headed out. *3:30 p.m. already. Dang, I really did get started late. I'll probably be one of the few heading this direction.* I started meeting people coming back from the glacier almost right away. A few people gave me nods and a couple said "hi," but many passed in silence.

Okay, that's enough silence. Time to play with seeing how many people engage when I say "hello." I reassured myself to quiet the nagging voice in my head that was trying to convince me not to do it. *It's not pushing cultural boundaries, and Gabriela did say people were more likely to engage in nature. This is also a safe culture. It's not like I'm in a bad area and putting myself in danger by engaging.* I felt the stubborn resolve growing in my core. *Besides, I bet over half the people here will be from cities, where the non-spoken speaking rules aren't as harsh, or from countries where people do engage more often. It's time to bring some balance between expressing my own self and my culture and honoring the culture I am in.*

"Heia," I greeted the next person I met on the trail, smiling at her and at myself for my decision.

"Heihei," she replied, smiling in return before bringing her focus back to the uneven path.

I bet the culture of hikers is especially open to saying hello and being friendly. How can a four-hour walk not make a person feel peaceful? I mean, unless they were dragged by someone else and are sore and grumpy, but even those people might enjoy a smile.

"Heia," I said to the couple I passed a few minutes later.

"Hi," they both replied in English.

Ha! I was suddenly very amused. *This will also be a fun game of trying to guess where people come from.* Buoyed by my new game and feeling lighter by these two small, yet significant-feeling connections, I trotted joyfully up the trail, humming to myself softly as I took in the beauty.

"Heia." I greeted the next couple coming my way. The man looked up from the trail with a huge smile and crossed the path in front of me with his hands extended. I felt myself quickly reach my hands out toward the warmth being offered.

"Buenos dias," he said, grasping my hand in a handshake, his other hand on the back of mine.

Oh, I love this! Greetings and touch together in such a genuine fashion. I could feel my chest lighten and my breath deepen. "Buenos dias, Señor!" I replied. *Ahhh.* My heart opened with the quick flood of joy. *It's amazing how just a small interaction with a stranger can create a happy little cocktail of feelings.*

He released his grasp and continued on his way. The woman behind him smiled broadly and nodded her greeting as she passed, attention on the roots below her feet.

See, Dawn! Many people do want to engage, or at least return a greeting to be polite. But judging by the smiles and body language, people on this trail are willing to engage. Perhaps some of those others, had I passed in silence, would have assumed I was ignoring them because of my own culture or desires. And how will I know who wants to connect if I do not make an effort? I am just opening the door to possibility.

I walked for another ten or fifteen minutes, greeting people as they passed, watching the reactions. Some gave what seemed like an automatic and offhanded response, but others smiled and engaged with ease.

Hiking the flat portion of the valley back from the glacier a few hours later, I noticed I was keeping pace with another guy, who was perhaps a quarter- or half-mile ahead of me.

Interesting. I knew there was a large tour group behind me, but I didn't see anyone else leave before me. Not thinking too much of it, I focused again on my step and the scenery, especially as the trail narrowed again between two valleys and became more steep and rocky. *There's probably not going to be anyone to interact with on the way back. It's too late in the evening.*

A while later, I turned a sharp bend in the trail to see it crossing the grey-blue waters of the glacial creek and then...

"BAAAAAAA!" An irritated momma sheep bleated and started coming toward me. *Whoa! Sheep are usually so intimidated. Her kids are over there, way upstream from me, and half-grown. She is overly-protective. Okay, I'll try to get past her by staying tight to the other side of the trail and not meeting her eyes.* She had the practical advantage though, as she had four legs and wasn't trying to keep her feet dry. "BAAAAAAA!!!" Her bell clanging, she kept coming as if she were going to cut me off at the pass.

"It's okay, so you can knock it off." I said gently out loud to her, keeping my head down and my focus on the rocks. "I'm not going to hurt you or your babies. There have been tons of people walking by you. Why are you so grumpy?"

I wonder if I am having a sheep equivalent of someone trying to talk down an attacking predator. I am unclear on what she would even do. Will she just come up and headbutt me? Will she bite? I cannot believe a stupid sheep is making me this nervous. I finished the crossing as she bleated at me again and trotted toward me. I picked up speed before noticing another short but deep crossing, where the man I had noticed earlier was standing. *Ooh, it looks like it is much worse crossing up there.* I scurried toward it anyway, trusting in my Keen hiking sandals to keep me secure as I tried to avoid the wrath of the mother sheep.

"Here." The man reached out his hand to help me.

"Thank you!" I exclaimed, taking it for the last few steps. "How weird. I haven't seen a sheep act that way before, especially when the lambs aren't exactly newborn."

"Yeah, she's been chasing me for a while up the trail. I had seen you behind me a while ago, and didn't want you to get blindsided by her. I have no idea if she would have attacked, but I wanted to make sure you got across okay."

"Well, thank you."

How considerate of him to think about my safety. That's often part of hiking culture, but it's great to be reaffirmed that people are still aware and attentive to others. Not only that, but he wasn't afraid to reach out a hand to help instead of just watching passively from afar.

We exchanged some chit-chat for a while. He was from Barcelona and with the tour group, but wanted to keep his own pace and take a couple of side trails before meeting up with the bus again. He stopped to gather water at the next site, and I kept going, revitalized by my restored faith in people's innate ability to create a sense of community, even on a one-to-one basis in the middle of a trail.

What a good reminder that I can open my awareness to people behind me as well, and that community and culture-building happens moment-to-moment. When everyone takes a bit of responsibility to be aware of others and meet them in a genuinely kind way, it encourages others to pay it forward as well. I thought about the camping group I'd experienced. *It's easy to walk into a place where the cultural norm is open communication and connection; but it takes a lot more effort and awareness to create it from scratch or to shift an already-existing culture by example.* I thought back about various times in my business and in my teaching career where I had been in a good place or a funk, and how my choices to communicate and connect slowly seeped into the cultural norms.

I remembered a streak in one of my massage classes where I had been pushing myself too hard. The class was always communicative and respectful with each other, and I felt I had a good connection with my students. *Then after I got sick that one week, I never really emotionally recovered. I felt disconnected and low-energy, and it showed in the way my students stopped reaching out to me. They also stopped working with each other so freely and started forming little mini-groups when they worked.* A bit of guilt washed over me as I realized how much impact I had on that mini-culture. *I really let them down. I didn't realize how drained I was at the time, but seeing the reflection in my students should have tipped me off that I was unintentionally shifting the class culture for the worse.* I took a deep breath. *I guess it can go either way. One person with a negative attitude can shift a culture to judgment, fear, and isolation, whereas one with a positive engaging attitude can shift the culture to one of collaboration and communication. Imagine what would happen if people mindfully added touch and the power of oxytocin to natural social bonding skills to create a sense of safety for others!*

I thought back to the lovely women's business group that made me feel accepted and warm and connected through their cultural norms.

Now that I think about it more clearly, there were a few groups I visited that didn't have that same vibe. They felt lower-energy, I didn't feel like I belonged, and it was tougher to connect with their leaders. When I spoke at one, a few women had complimented me, saying that it was one of the most fun meetings they had; but I bet it was the group of friends who came to support me and their high-energy that tipped the scales even more than the presentation.

It made sense. The more people that come together to choose the cultural norm, the faster the culture can shift.

There is great power in numbers, intention, and safety. It may take a bit more effort and energy than working on it from the top down, but it can easily start with one person reaching out to make a change.

I thought back to a couple of interviews I had done in preparation for my book, in which I asked the question: What do you think is the biggest thing that prevents people from touching others in their communities? The answers varied from "cultural taboos" to "being afraid of offending someone and invading someone else's space" to "being more self-aware rather than aware of others around them, especially strangers or when in an unfamiliar environment. It takes a confident individual to be more aware of others and what respectful touch looks like in those situations."

Up until yesterday you have fallen dead in the center, Dawn. You have been so concerned with what others will think, you disconnected from yourself again and allowed fear to rule. Instead of bridging gaps purposefully, you stood back to evaluate and did nothing, and then regretted it once it was too late to engage. But you changed all of that today. I smiled and gave myself a little pat on the back.

Awareness comes first. Being aware and intentional of the culture we want to create for ourselves and perhaps even recruiting others around us is the first step. My mind flashed back to another time when I had unintentionally shifted the culture of interactions to the negative. *Uugh. I wish I'd had more presence when my mom came to visit me in August.*

Campfires and Conversations

Goodness, Göteborg Airport is loud. The bustle of people and sound of overhead announcements were half the intensity of major airports like Chicago, New Jersey, Stockholm, and Brussels; but two months in the quiet Norwegian countryside had left me sensitive to visual input, sounds, and people. After grabbing my bags I took the local bus to the hostel, positioning myself so I could see the lights of the city as we drove through it. *I'm glad it's not very crowded on the bus. I don't have to worry about hogging seats with my rucksack and laptop case.* An odd sound drifted up from the back of the bus. *Oh, it's someone singing quietly and a bit off-key to some music. How funny!* I grinned, happy about the freedom this person was expressing.

"Sir. Excuse me." A loud male British voice interrupted my moment of joy. "Sir, please stop singing."

Oh, he's not that loud, and he's only singing a few bars here and there. It's not like he's belting out a whole tune. He's not bothering anyone.

I watched the hectic airport life drift away as we drove toward the equally busy city. My thoughts turned to what I wanted to do in the morning before I picked up the rental car and my mom from the airport I had just left.

"Sir!" The angry voice broke my train of thought. "Sir, this is NOT your living room. PLEASE! Be quiet. No more singing."

Dude. You are more obnoxious than the singer. I turned around, curious at the events unfolding behind me. I was getting agitated at this man's response and the fact that he had no idea that his obnoxious attitude was significantly more disruptive than the singing.

Yep. Way more sensitive than normal. Usually I'd just be able to ignore it, but now I almost want to intervene— just to shut the yeller up. My stomach tightened at the rudeness. *If I hadn't just come from such a quiet culture, I'd probably turn around and tell him to move if he didn't like it. But right now, it feels challenging to even hear the conflict without engaging in it.*

The concept that I was acting different because of the culture I just left hit me, and I pondered how my body and mind were trying to process all I was experiencing.

It's really no different than people with touch. If people are used to a lot of touch and get it all the time, it can be no big deal. It's not something that stands out in their day-to-day life; whereas if someone only gets touched once a month, that touch can be immensely impactful and maybe even overwhelming. The busyness of the city and all the input in my system is overwhelming me the same way. I know I will adjust to it, the same way I have adjusted to not receiving much touch.

I made it to the city hostel without incident, found my dorm room, and crawled into bed. *Uugh. I've never had the breathing of others bother me before. And I don't think I remembered to pack my eye mask and earplugs.* I tried to meditate and focus on my breath, as the sound of someone rolling over reached my ears. *I was more accustomed to the gentle sound of the creek and the absolute silence than I thought. Last year I could fall asleep to snoring. I guess this is good practice for the three weeks I'll be in the same room with my mom.* But finally my meditation calmed my mind and my fatigue carried me off into sleep.

Eight hours later, feeling rested, I greeted my mom at the airport.

"Welcome to Göteborg, Mom!" I exclaimed joyfully as she walked up to me, opening my arms for a long hug and a kiss on the cheek. "How was your flight?" My body was warm and cozy with the idea that we'd have the opportunity to hang out for three weeks. *That should mean a lot of hugs and talking and feel-good hormones, which I've been missing out on during my travels. And I can catch up on the people back home. We'll be traveling a lot, but after being in one spot for two months, it will be a nice change of pace.* The extrovert in me had missed the faster pace of people and easy communication with strangers, even though I was still adjusting to it. *Now, for a quick seventy-minute drive to Kajsa's house, and all will be good.*

We caught up on the way to Kajsa's, stopping to eat a proper dinner.

"You are going to love Kajsa and her family," I told her across the table full of knäckebröd, toast skagen, herring, and salmon. "They are so friendly and warm. They made me feel like family when I was there over Christmas last year."

"You mentioned that," my mom said, "and I cannot wait to meet her. I brought her a special chocolate gift from Whitman's candy in Crookston."

"And, Kajsa is a hugger—I know you love that!"

We laughed together, appreciating my mom's strong love of hugs and family. I had always loved hearing the story of how when she first got engaged to my dad, she started hugging his family and telling them she loved them.

I can't imagine not having had that bond.

We arrived at Kajsa's, and after a round of hugs and snacks, Mom announced she was ready for bed.

"What?" I said playfully, "Your body only thinks it's two in the afternoon. You can't be tired."

She rolled her eyes in jest. "Yeah, I guess I'll just skip a whole night's sleep. I don't think you want me that grumpy tomorrow."

After goodnight hugs she headed upstairs, and Kajsa and I caught up a bit more before I went upstairs to unpack and settle in, even though I was feeling restless.

I really want to do some writing. It's been a few days, and I am so close to being done. Wouldn't it be great if I could finish the rough draft of the book before mid-September? I pulled out my laptop and promptly got distracted with emails, sales tax, and client scheduling. An hour later I looked at the clock. *Ugh. I better get to bed so I can have energy for tomorrow and get myself aligned on time with my mom like last time. Our flow goes so much better when we are on the same schedule.* I climbed into bed and lay there, awake and restless and thinking about all I could be doing. *Stop it, Dawn,* I chided myself. *You have plenty of time to get all of this done. Heck, you can work on it at night when your mom goes to bed for a couple of hours. Even that should be enough to make good progress so you can finish it quickly when she leaves.* That must have been enough to settle my mind, as I quickly drifted off to sleep.

The next several days were filled with walks and conversation. I made sure to bring her to a few spots I enjoyed but also to experience new and different places together so we could create memories. I did most of the driving so she could absorb the scenery, and kept to my own night-owl schedule to focus on my book while she slept.

It kind of feels like I'm just doing to do, and that I'm really not present with her. I sat overlooking the water in front of Kajsa's house, pondering the last few days of activity before leaving. I thought back to a comment my mom had made earlier in the day about hoping she wasn't pulling me away from my book. *She senses my disconnect and is trying to reach out. I need to do a better job engaging with her. After all, she came here on vacation so we could play together. I know I've changed a lot, but my playfulness is still in here.* I jumped online and peeked at TripAdvisor, looking for something new to do on the way to our next destination near the Gota Kanal. *I should find something fun for us to do together so we can reconnect again. She will go explore on her own while I work tomorrow night. The day is the time to really focus on our connection.*

With a few places marked and mapped out, I hopped into bed, ready for whatever the next day would bring us.

"What a great find!" Mom exclaimed the next afternoon, looking around the park where we sat on my sarong, lunch laid out in front of us and acoustic music from the local farmer's market drifting through the trees. "Walking along that marsh was beautiful, and this food you packed is great. Thank you for getting everything together."

"No problem." I was enjoying myself, glad to be hearing live music outdoors and spending some relaxing time with my mom. *Yes, I feel grounded and connected today. I'm glad. I was a bit worried about myself and my inability to connect with her. Though I have been a bit irritable today in the car. I need to be careful of that. I want more connection on a deeper level before I go off by myself again for the next three months. It really shouldn't be too hard.* But the nagging feeling that something was missing didn't leave me, and I found myself on edge and distracted nonetheless for the next few days.

One morning Mom rolled over and snuggled next to me. *Aw. That feels so nice. I'm sure she's touch-deprived because she's used to being cuddled with my dad.* I snuggled closer to her, relishing the connection, even as I was bombarded by the details of the day and wondering about the lack of response in my body. *It feels nice, but it's like my body isn't releasing the hormones. Like I'm mentally overriding the good stuff with my stress stuff. Didn't I read a report that indicated that being distracted could interrupt the positive benefits of touch? I suppose that's what's happening.*

I snuggled in closer and gave myself a little pep talk. *You are falling into the routine of non-communication with loved ones and taking the situation for granted. Talk to her today and find that connection with her. You've withdrawn a bit out of habit and because things aren't flowing easily. Let her know what's going on. And if the book isn't flowing, just go to bed. Stop distracting yourself with finding things you could do with her and just be in the moment. That's what she's here for. Vacation and to be with you.*

Mom rolled over and got up, heading toward the bathroom.

See? You weren't even present for that because you were so mind-chattery. Knock it off.

Later in the day, I noticed I was being grumpy again in the car and took the opportunity to talk with her as well as reset myself. "Sorry I'm so grumpy. I don't know what is going on with me." I said, looking at her while she drove down the road. "I really want to have fun, and I think I'm just taking things out on you."

"I've noticed, honey," she replied. "Is everything okay? I know you wanted to finish your book and it seems like it's been frustrating for you."

"Yeah, but it feels deeper than that though—like I'm discontent for no reason, and I can't really get into a comfortable place in my body. I want you to know I'm glad you are here; and I am having a good time, and hope you are, too."

"Yes. And I appreciate you are doing so much work and research finding things for us to do and making all the plans."

Wow. Somehow I didn't think she had noticed. That she had taken it for granted that I was doing all of that.

I paused for a few moments. "Well, I'll do better." I promised, vowing internally to hold my end of the bargain.

I don't want to continue this way any longer. Neither one of us feels really satisfied or settled like this. Even though it's not as easy as usual, I've worked with harder glitches in relationships.

Yet a few days later the feeling was still with me. I thought about another interview in which I had asked how people could overcome the hesitation of reaching out to others. Their answer was "Be aware of the amount of time alone and with others." The answer reinforced exactly what was happening.

Oh! I went from all alone to only with my mom. I have only had alone time at night while she is sleeping, but I haven't been using it to recharge myself.

We were on the last leg of the trip, and had arrived in a suburb of Slagsta, a working-class factory city and a suburb of Stockholm. When we walked into the simple studio the lack of color, decoration, and hominess resonated with the bare energy I felt emotionally.

I just cannot shake this. I wanted to reach out, to hug more, to cuddle; yet when she reached out to me, I could tell what I gave her was flat and devoid of connection. *How can I be so disconnected? I know I am feeling her sensitivity to the disconnect as well, which isn't helping.* Guilt overwhelmed me as I gave myself the burden and blame of ruining her vacation with my moodiness. *Stop it. We have had some great times. It is just different than normal. It doesn't make it wrong. Remember, you are doing the best you can with the energy you have right now.* It had improved since our last conversation, but it was far from what I craved. *It's time to integrate this work within myself and find a happy balance, both with my communications with my mom and with other people.*

"Hey, Mom?" I reached out hesitantly.

"What do you need, honey?" She asked, hearing the question and the regret in my voice.

"I'm sorry I have been so distant on this trip so far. I thought it would get better, but it hasn't yet. But I'm really going to be intentional in the last week to stay present, okay? I love you and I want us to be playful together again."

"Yes, we have been running hard, unlike the last time we traveled together," my mom pointed out. "I think we both have been a bit worn out. It's okay." She came over and gave me a lovely reassuring hug.

Mmmmmmm. Now I feel all snuggly and proper. Simple communication can really go a long way in fixing things.

Deepening Campfire Conversations

I had another opportunity to practice a few weeks later after my mom headed home. I entered my friend Diana's one-bedroom flat after being gone all day at an Upledger CranioSacral class and a long workout and immediately felt the sadness in the air. *Something is really wrong.* I took off my laptop and went down the narrow hall to the kitchen to fill up my water bottle before walking into the living room to meet her.

I hope she's not upset with me for not spending much time with her while I'm here, but assisting this class is taking up so much time and energy; and I have to do some level of exercise before coming home or I will get sore and physically restless and won't sleep.

"Today was a really rough day." Diana said to me, slumped on her couch in the living room where I was sleeping for a few days. I sat on the chair adjacent to her and watched her silently. "I couldn't get a hold of my daughter for over twenty-four hours, and I found out our friend Sarah's breast cancer has spread into her lungs."

Wow. No wonder. Two big hits in the same day. Her twenty-three-year-old daughter had been in constant communication while in India. *I swear they are usually chatting or messaging every hour or so.*

"Twenty-four years old and that level of cancer," she continued in a disconnected, emotionless tone. "I don't know what to think. Can that even be cured?" She looked at me blankly, hoping I had some answer.

"I don't know much about that type of cancer or her level. I'm really sorry, Diana." The trumpeting noise of the anchorwoman's voice clashed harshly with the sad quietness of the cold room.

I want to go give her a giant hug and reassure her and let her know everything will be okay. But I know that sometimes people just need to feel. I'll let her take the lead and keep checking in.

"I am in shock. I don't know what to do." She shifted her gaze from mine and stared at the television's garish light.

"Is your daughter okay? Nothing bad happened to her, right?" I prompted hopefully, knowing if it had, it would have been mentioned already.

"Yeah, she's okay. Just in as much shock as me, I guess." Diana picked up her phone and started texting again as I waited and held space the best I could.

"What can I do? What do you need? Shall I make dinner?" I prompted her for ways I could support.

Why didn't I ask if she would like a hug? Hmm. That's interesting. I feel her pain from here. It feels like my heart is being squeezed, and all I want to do is tear up. But I don't want to push her. She obviously wants some space and to engage with her family on the phone.

"Yeah, dinner's already ready," she said offhandedly. "It needs something. See if you can figure it out. I just can't focus."

I went into the kitchen and tasted the sauce. *Tastes good, maybe a bit of pepper for spice once we put it on the pasta.* I stirred it as I added some, noting it was getting stuck on the bottom. *Shit. I scraped off burned stuff. Now it all tastes burnt. Way to be helpful.* The internal sarcasm and self-criticism was getting strong fast. *Hmm. I don't know what to do for her and I'm feeling useless and irritable at myself. Interesting.* I made two platefuls and brought the food to her. She took it mechanically and started eating. We finished in silence and she continued to text and watch tv for the next two television shows.

I am so bored and restless. TV kills me. She doesn't want to engage. I should get some work done anyway. I pulled out my computer and opened it to my class links. *I'll keep an eye on her and stay open if she wants to talk. I know she's leaving at 5 a.m. so I'll give her hugs then if she's ready for them.*

The next morning came quickly, and she rushed about getting things organized to go.

"Diana, can I carry something out to the car for you? Make you coffee? How can I help?" She still seemed sad and disconnected, even in her rush. *Uugh. I feel like I'm just in her way.* I sat down and started playing with the kitten, hoping at least to keep it from getting underfoot in the hustle as the dog came up hoping for scratches behind the ears.

"Okay, I'm loading the animals and I'm out," she said, rushing into the living room. I scooped up the kitten and put him in the carrier.

"I'll grab the cat for you," I said, slipping on my shoes.

We rushed out to the car and she turned to go.

"Diana, can I give you a hug before you go? I really appreciate everything and you letting me stay here."

I hope she can feel my gratitude through her state. I really want to help her in some way.

"Yep, alright," she said, turning and giving me a long hug before jumping in her car.

I watched her pull away, regret already creeping in.

I said that wrong. I meant to ask if she would like one— one for her, not for me. It was intended to be for her. I don't feel like I did enough for her and supported her well. Maybe she didn't notice the wording, and I hope she felt my intent through her fog, but who knows. I turned back toward the flat, a little defeated.

See—you are trying to teach this to people and keep doing it wrong yourself. The self-criticism got brutal. *You should just knock it off and stop reaching out.*

Suddenly my resolve strengthened again as I realized my reptilian brain was screwing with me and trying to keep me safe. *Nope. It's all a learning process. I'm not going to be perfect at this. No one is. The point is to do the best we can to make connection and communicate; and if we screw up in a way that offends another, to take responsibility and make amends the best we can. That's the only way communities and relationships can grow. So shut up, brain.*

Feeling suddenly lighter and more energetic, I closed the door behind me and went back to the couch for an early morning nap.

Rainbows Emerge After Rain

As I pondered my next phase in life while eating lunch later that afternoon, a voice broke through my reverie. "Hi there. How's your meal? It looks interesting." The gentleman in his mid-eighties addressed a woman sitting alone at a table near the door in the small café. She looked at him puzzled, mouth full of food. "Oops, sorry, I guess you are eating," he said, patting her shoulder before navigating the narrow spaces between the tables and buffet to move further into the modest space. He grabbed the placemat menu off another table, and looked at it inquisitively as the waiter came over.

"Would you like a table, sir?" the waiter inquired. "It's all you can eat for £7.50, and you can order any of those drinks for an extra charge." He gestured at the menu now clutched beneath the old man's arm.

"I don't know how much I can eat," the older gentleman, cane in one hand, put his free hand on the waiter's upper arm. "I need to look things over." He turned to gaze toward the buffet offerings and started chatting with the people in queue, all of whom seemed a bit stunned by his abrupt entrance and energy.

How lovely. People don't know how to take him, but he is just trying to connect. When he looked up in my direction I smiled at him. *People are treating him like "some old guy" and aren't really engaging. It's such a shame that older people seem to be treated like a bother.* Catching my smile, he walked over to me.

"The food is good," I said in introduction. "Quite the variety and really fresh."

"Yeah? I'll have to take another look." He wandered back over to the buffet as I stood up to get my second round. "What is in this, do you think?" he asked, pointing at a beef dish.

"It's all up on the wall there," I gestured to signs hung above the front picture window that I hadn't seen myself until I was eating.

He patted my arm and rested his hand there briefly, almost as if he was stabilizing himself. "I think I'll eat here," he declared and then sat himself at the nearest table.

What a friendly guy, I thought as I plopped back down at my table, plate piled with a variety of veggie salads and some Caribbean chicken. *It makes me happy we could connect for a moment. I was in such a funk today, and even that little bit of connection made me smiley inside.*

"Look, he's eating here because of you," the woman at the table next to me noted. "He is so sweet. I often wonder what my dad would have been like at that age."

We watched him together as he reached out to get the attention of a passing waitress, thanking her for bringing him such cold water and ice. *Hmm, she shrunk back a bit. I wonder if she was surprised? Or if she found his gesture inappropriate?*

"He's just trying to connect with people, isn't he?" she asked me, the nostalgic tone still in her voice. "I think you made his day."

"Yes, I wish others would see him simply as a human looking for connection, instead of brushing him aside because he's half-deaf and maybe a bit too touchy for today's culture."

"I hope you keep being positive and engaging. We all need to do more of that." She stood to leave, putting her colorful purse over her shoulder and tucking her curly hair behind her ears. "Have a lovely day."

That makes me feel warm inside, but I wonder if she would have reached out like that too? Especially after she mentioned her dad. I pondered for a second how we interact with elderly people. *There is such an increase of loneliness in the older population, as we separate as families.* I had read about how the older people get, the more they want to be touched; but the opportunity to be touched by friends and family gets markedly reduced because people do not like touching older people.[62] *My dad has commented that he touches and hugs his friends now more than he ever did when he was younger. He credits my generation for bringing more touch forward, but I wonder if that is true? Or perhaps they touch within their own generation, but younger people don't reach out to them?*

I sat pondering the absence of touch in people of all ages who are socially isolated and/or lonely until my body alerted me to the present moment. *I am still hungry after that workout. Maybe my body needs more protein.* I wandered up to the buffet for my third round, pausing by the older man's table on the way. "What do you think? Is it good, or did I mislead you?" I grinned at him, noting that he had already eaten over half of his plate.

"Good, thank you," he replied, green eyes sparkling as he reached out to pat my arm again. "Lovely food."

He's so happy right now. Even if no one knows what to do with him, I'm glad I was here to reach out.

I finished my final plate, paid at the counter at the back of the café, and started to leave.

"You have a lovely and wonderful day, my dear," he said, reaching out both his hands to clasp mine.

"I will! Are you from around here?" I asked, sensing he would appreciate more conversation.

I have all the time in the world. Why let this little bit of connection be all it is? Why not spend a few more minutes chatting?

I sat down facing him, my arms on the table as he introduced himself as Armond and started talking about his wife and his extended family.

He's super funny. I love that he is so obviously proud of what his wife is doing.

"If you are going to Cornwall, maybe you should go on one of my wife's trips!" he exclaimed, grabbing my arm enthusiastically and then patting it again. "Wow, you are warm! Warm arms, warm heart. I know you've warmed mine."

My heart is melting. What luck to have picked this café today.

I giggled, placing my hand on his. "I have really enjoyed chatting with you," I said genuinely. "It's always nice to learn a bit from strangers, eh?"

I have learned a bit, I noted, surprised. *It's been a while since I watched someone so genuinely and innocently touch others. By today's standards many would consider him completely inappropriate, but it's like he sees everyone in the café as a friend and is touching respectfully for what he knows. I'm sure I could debate with many women about how he needs to learn boundaries, but why can't they be the ones to speak up and set their own boundaries? To gently ask him not to touch them, but still talk.* I shook my head slightly, thinking of the crisis of it all. *Generationally, humans don't communicate well.*

After our "goodbyes," I left the café and wandered down the street and thought about my friend's dad who said that the older he got, the more invisible and insignificant he felt in public.

Wouldn't it be great if we stepped up our awareness and communication cross-generationally and started using touch as a respectful way to reconnect and bond? I hope the work I'm doing can facilitate that.

I smiled to myself, remembering a woman who contacted me a couple weeks after I gave a talk on using touch to include people. "I've started asking the people I see during Meals on Wheels if they want a hug before I go!" she shared excitedly. "Most take me up on it, and a couple have commented they haven't hugged anyone in a long time and how nice it is."

So much power in one simple question, one simple act. Mother Teresa was so right when she said, "Not all of us can do great things. But we can do small things with great love."

I can't wait to finish this book and facilitate others' communication as well. 2020 is going to be a big year of change for me and so many others. Not only do I get to bring even stronger touch communication to my relationships; but as I re-enter my communities, I can consciously rebuild them and help form a new culture.

I took a deep breath and turned to walk to the sea, envisioning my journey home a few weeks ahead and the stories I would share.

Did You Know?

"Warm climates tend to produce cultures that are more liberal about touching than colder regions (think Greeks versus Germans, or Southern hospitality versus New England stoicism). There are a number of hypotheses as to why, including the fact that a higher ambient temperature increases the availability of skin."[63]

People deprived of affection have higher rates of "loneliness, depression, stress, alexithymia, preoccupied and fearful avoidant attachment styles, and numbers of personality disorders, mood and anxiety disorders, and secondary immune disorders."[64]

An observational 1973 study found, "In any communication, who initiates touch is a clear indicator of social status. It seems that all humans follow some unsaid rules; wherein, the person with higher status chooses whether touch becomes a part of the communication. This status could be derived from sex, race, age, or socioeconomic status. When persons of the same 'status' interact, touch is used as a sign of solidarity and acceptance."[65]

Community Remedies
Languages Share Common Roots

Throughout most of this book I've been talking about an individual's journey to integrating more touch for themselves; but this chapter is focused on the process of bringing touch into smaller cultures and communities like families, workplaces, social settings, etc. As you can see from my stories, people of different ages, cultures, and backgrounds can have different touch needs, expectations, fears, assumptions, and judgments. Instead of separating people out or ignoring these differences, we can approach it with a sense of awareness and a child-like curiosity. Have you ever noticed that people growing up in the same family household can emerge with completely different personalities, attitudes, and perceptions? The same goes with touch in various social, work, spiritual, economic, and physical cultures. Although there may be similarities of beliefs, and it may be helpful to categorize for simplicity, each individual is unique and will have strengths and challenges around healthy touch and communication based upon their own life experiences and programming.

With all the papers, books, and research I have read and the people I have talked to, one thing is clear. Touch is a complicated issue and tricky terrain to navigate. It will likely take some time and devotion to cultivate cultures in which we are communicating and touching other people in ways that increase safety, deepen healthy connection and trust, improve our health with more oxytocin and serotonin and less cortisol, enhance our emotional well-being and mood, and decrease violence in our communities. After years of touch feeling unsafe and even taboo, honoring and respecting ourselves and each other again will not happen overnight. As my friend Frank, a former psychologist, said to me one day, "I believe we're all longing to connect. At least when I believe everyone in the room is longing to connect, connecting is easy."

Know the Culture

The conversation can incorporate many aspects of the culture including values, geography, stage of life, social conditioning, and leadership. It's important to note how cultural values add another level to our own personal touch-awareness. I have many male friends who have good touch communication, but I find other men in Western culture seem to fear touch. Gender roles, our current fear culture, and societal programming have made it less acceptable for men to need or ask for touch. Many of the messages men get around needing touch imply it is weak to need it or that any touch they give or receive is sexual, no matter what gender they identify with or who they are touching. There is also a push in the culture for men to be aware and consensual when they touch, which is appropriate; but the resources and grace to teach them how to do all of that is lacking. Perhaps that is why so many men are seeking out massage and professional cuddling instead of pursuing it in social situations. As mentioned, men shared the same bed with strangers in early American taverns while traveling. Unfortunately, many in our culture would look at the same actions today as unacceptable; yet this culture is slowly changing as well. One 2017 study found:

> 30 heterosexual undergraduate males interviewed felt safer cuddling, hugging and, especially, confiding in platonic male friends than they did with their girlfriends...[they] provided less judgment and increased emotional stability, enhanced emotional disclosure, social fulfillment, and better conflict resolution, compared to the emotional lives they shared with girlfriends.[66]

In Arab countries, parts of Asia, and some Southern European cultures, men hold hands walking down the street in friendship and to show mutual respect.

A study of over 500 adults from 17 countries found there was "no strong correlation with age or ethnicity, but men reported a significantly higher affection deprivation on average than women."[67]

Touch habits vary widely culture-to-culture geographically as well. In Latin America it is common to kiss on the cheek as a greeting, whereas in Japan a bow or head nod is the accepted standard. In Muslim cultures, cross-gender touch is forbidden in public. Even in European cultures some people kiss once, some twice, and some three times on the cheek, depending on region and familiarity with the other.

The larger culture in parts of Northern Europe and the U.S. have unwritten rules that have made us touch-phobic and touch-judgmental. These have expanded into practices that dictate how we react to touch as well as our level of sensitivity and outrage if we perceive someone's actions to be inappropriate—even if that person has no idea s/he has offended. Instead of a generous assumption and firm redirect, we are being taught to feel violated and angry. That being said, I do realize people have their limits. For example, I often hear about women who touch another pregnant woman's belly or her baby without asking permission. The first happened often enough to one friend that she vowed, "The next woman who walks up and two-handed grabs my belly without my permission is going to get her tits grabbed in response." Bald people and people of color often have their head or hair touched without permission as well. I believe our whole culture will thrive as we train ourselves to be thoughtful and respectful and, when others forget to, respond with a firm redirect instead of a lashing. Remember, you cannot always choose what happens to you, but you can *always* choose how you respond.

Healthy touch builds trust and helps us connect. Think about the last time you sat in a crowded theater or bus next to someone you did not know. Did you allow your body to touch the person next to you? Why or why not? Where did that come from? Most people in the U.S. avoid touching others unless they want to connect with them or unless the bus takes a sharp curve. In contrast, in

India people have no compunction about having bodies touch each other. With our rules and fears perhaps we haven't even considered another possibility. Or perhaps, unconsciously, we are aware that touch connects people; and that to be connected, even in such a small way is scary/ exciting/ uncomfortable/ confusing/ unsafe/ comforting/ intimidating/ compelling; and we do not want to be judged, criticized, or scolded. We also have preconceptions and unconscious biases around who and what is safe based upon our own and others' age, gender identity, race and economic status.

The phase of life someone is in can also dictate their need for or aversion to touch. Many mothers of young children report being overwhelmed by the amount and type of touch in their lives; whereas elderly folks tend to want or need more touch, especially after losing a partner or as their family has less time for tactile interactions. However, loneliness and social isolation are not limited to the older generations.

While I traveled on my own for months, beyond experiencing and engaging with the cultures in which I was immersed, I had many opportunities to experience both social isolation and loneliness. The two didn't seem completely linked, as I was sometimes—but not often—lonely when socially isolated. The article "Social Isolation, Loneliness in Older People Pose Health Risks" delineates the difference. "Social isolation is the objective physical separation from other people (living alone), while loneliness is the subjective distressed feeling of being alone or separated. It's possible to feel lonely while among other people, and you can be alone yet not feel lonely."[68]

One can be surrounded by people and still feel lonely, or can be socially isolated and not feel lonely at all. I know many in our culture feel acute loneliness and try to fill it with things like work, internet browsing, alcohol, exercise, and being around people, even if they do not feel connected to them. Clients report over and over again feeling separate from their friends, families, and colleagues. Even children as young as five or six have a basic understanding of loneliness.

The "show of happiness" over social media can enhance this. One can easily look through Facebook, Instagram, or the social media of choice, and find evidence that "everyone else" is happy, popular, successful, connected to their friends, in a great marriage/relationship, and so on while we are alone and struggling with no one to lean on or no one that is knocking down our door insisting we take their help/support/love/money, etc. Studies of the quality of online interactions in adolescents are divided as to whether they lead to deeper or shallower social relationships; although creating online friendships was related to a motivation to compensate for lack of social support.[69]

There are many studies trying to correlate the actions of our younger generations around social media. Many self-report being lonely, and scientists are trying to determine if loneliness drives them to social media or if social media is partly driving the loneliness—because the connections are not always as genuine, and the opportunity for bullying exists. Most studies I found show trends, but are inconclusive.

Conceivably, our loneliness is related not only to a lack of deeper personal connection, but also to the lack of the feel-good hormones released by touch: oxytocin, serotonin, and dopamine. I have noticed that correlation within me, and have observed clients and friends reporting more loneliness when they feel deprived of physical affection. Articles abound on how to become more connected with others, the importance of bringing touch into one's life, the negative impact phones and social media have on our social connection, and even how *not* to touch.

So why aren't we having the harder conversations and embracing opportunities to connect? I do not know what would have happened if I had snubbed Armond in the café or freaked out on him because he touched my arm. I do not know if any of the people he has touched along the way have been traumatized or fearful or scared or if they have they been like me. I do know that by working on my own shame, fears, and social conditioning around touch I have been able to find these places of connection, healing, and joy and help others to do the same.

And that is my hope for you as an individual who is part of many cultures and sub-cultures.

Become a Leader

As a leader in your own community and subcultures, you can create small, steady, and powerful changes by using your (perhaps newfound; perhaps expanded) touch and communication skills. As you release your fears, you can begin to consciously choose your actions and reactions, as well as decide how to safely and respectfully push and pull the culture around you into healthier interactions.

This book has offered some gentle ways to gain consent around touch, while also tuning you into your own touch hang-ups, sensitivities (or lack-thereof) and challenges. The key to addressing the touch crisis in our culture/communities/organizations/groups is to hold both the awareness of self and the awareness of the cultures we engage. The question to ask yourself is "How can I comfortably and safely integrate touch into my life to benefit myself and my communities (school, family system, workplace, social settings, volunteer spaces, etc.)?" Then, collaborate with others and decide how the journey toward healthier touch in that community can be brought about in a safe and respectful way. Remember my experience on the hike? That's what I was doing. I was trying to bridge my own need for connection in a healthy way in a culture that was not extremely touch-forward.

You can begin to gently pull your culture by adding bits of healthy touch. Look back at your commitments to touch in chapters three and four, and expand those to a broader audience. Sit with people you have relationships with, and bring intentional conversations around touch to rekindle connection the way I did with my mom. Be curious and even clumsy at first. Acknowledge your need for touch and explore the wording that suits you, the way I did with Alan. Show compassion and offer touch to someone in need, the way Charlie did for me.

How you choose to gently push your individual cultures and shape them can have long-lasting impact not only for you, but for the physical and emotional health of others.

Touch Regulations versus Active Communication

If in your culture you are attempting to create more trust, more communication, and more openness, perhaps playing a bit of "devil's advocate" to someone who is reacting strongly to being touched—or asking him/her to reflect if there was any form of communication around the unwanted touch—can help bring awareness and responsibility. Opening a conversation about how creating a culture of communication around touch is more productive than a straight no-touch rule.

Rules restricting touch could potentially have a negative consequence for personal relationships, trust, and confidence in the culture. For example, when I went to a meditation course there was a no-touch rule, which worked fine and was functional during the meditation days. However, at the end of the ten-day course when people were talking and the rules had all been relaxed, except for touch, we found ourselves wanting to hug each other goodbye, to touch each other on the arm to gain attention and to genuinely connect through touch after such a hard and emotional journey together. Not being able to touch for fear of getting in trouble created an awkwardness—a discomfort that many felt. I heard many people say "I would love to give you a hug, but..." or "I wish I could hug you, but I don't want to get in trouble." I would overhear people apologize "Oops, sorry. I forgot we are not supposed to touch." I am sure there were some people at the end who welcomed the excuse to not involve physical contact; but for many of us it served to create a division, a separation, and a barrier to closer connection.

Start bringing the larger conversation about healthy touch into your childrens' lives and into their classrooms and social circles. The conversation about touch deserves to be so much larger than "good touch, bad touch." Cultivating your child's ability to speak up for his or her own body boundaries will carry much further beyond the potential for abuse. It is a skill that will help them in relationships of all kinds as well as teach them to speak up for themselves in other arenas of life. One Youth Services Law blog post stated the following:

The other problem with no-touch policies is that they prevent kids from learning what appropriate touch looks like, especially if those kids do not receive enough physical affection at home. Kids need to practice physical touch among themselves and with adults to learn what is appropriate, and to learn how to read the body language of the person receiving their touch. This is body language that will inform them whether their touch is welcome or not, and it is crucial to learning how to set boundaries within any interaction.[70]

When our children can have healthy touch within safe communities—including with teachers and other children—and are taught about healthy touch boundaries, we set them up for increased brain development, enhanced growth, better immune systems, increased self-esteem, and the potential for stronger social bonds. Plus, it sets them up to learn to say their *no* strongly when they enter their dating years, and hear others' *nos* as well.

As Brené Brown said in her book, *Rising Strong*, "It often takes just a single brave person to change the trajectory of a family, or of any system, for that matter."[71]

If your culture does not say what is appropriate and inappropriate, each individual has to make his/her best guess, which can be even more scary and awkward (unless you are putting these concepts of clearer communication and consent into practice). One poll suggested some people want touch banned in the workplace to avoid "awkward greetings," but stated: "Having guidelines which facilitate open, honest conversations between workers about physical contact offers employers the chance to have their team focused on the job at hand rather than whether they're shaking hands at their next meeting."[72]

The added benefit to encouraging conversations is the creation of cultural skills and positive habits that can carry across communication in all areas of the organization. In fact, not every organization currently sees touch in the workplace as threatening. If we can do this with pronouns, as we see in some places of business and schools, we could surely do it with touch language. Don't you think?

Research from Robert Half affiliate, The Creative Group, surveyed 400 U.S. advertising and marketing managers and found "65 percent of advertising and marketing managers surveyed said it's at least somewhat common to hug coworkers. And 52 percent said the same regarding clients and business contacts."[73]

Perhaps your culture can collaborate to create touch guidelines that help form the structure without limiting it. Examples may include the following:
- Gain consent before touching.
- Handshakes are appropriate unless requested otherwise.

- Give the person the benefit of the doubt the first time you are touched in a way you don't like and clearly communicate what you would prefer.
- Be mindful of power differentials, and allow the person with lesser power to reach out to the person in higher power. (Unspoken social power differentials also still unfortunately exist, and some guidelines may need to exist for this as well such as gender identity, race, nationality, class, etc.)
- Do not take it personally if someone does not engage in physical contact with you.
- Feel free to change how you interact with touch in the culture at any time, but please clearly communicate your needs.
- Honor the strictest boundaries at all times.

I know people who work in a professional theater, and there is a huge culture of positive touch. However, the administrative organization started imposing guidelines and policies which clashed with the culture and made people feel uncomfortable and awkward. Some cultures are already self-regulating and need minimal, if any, adjustments.

Sometimes a culture will find its own way to communicate touch, regardless of policy. For example, a chaplain in Wisconsin told me about his work in juvenile detention facilities. When no-touch policies were implemented, many females still wanted to console each other. They developed a special "hug" in which they would hug themselves, put their hands on their shoulders—then touch elbows.

Teaching people to communicate about touch teaches them to communicate better elsewhere. You are opening the door to openness, honesty, and a potential for better and more functional working relationships. There may still be awkward moments and conflict or someone who is not following rules. There will be people who make mistakes as they learn, and people who flagrantly ignore the rule for whatever reason. The point is, these things will happen with or without no-touch policies in place, so why don't we open ourselves to the possibility and work toward collaboration?

An Internal Peek

How many different cultures do you interact with (i.e. subcultures, communities, organizations, groups, workplaces, etc.)?

Definitions of culture:

5. the behaviors and beliefs characteristic of a particular social, ethnic, or age group.

6. *Anthropology.* the sum total of ways of living built up by a group of human beings and transmitted from one generation to another.[74]

Here are some ways for you to begin bringing the conversation and experience into your culture.

First, Remember Your Cultural Touch Roots

In chapter one, I asked you to look at your beliefs and roots around touch. When you apply your belief structure to the cultures in your past, what do you notice? Did your belief come from a characteristic of the subculture(s) you were exposed to? Was it passed generationally? Or were you conditioned around touch to display excellent behaviors and manners? What did the culture teach you and why, and how do you overcome whatever is remaining that no longer suits you?

Second, Practice What You've Learned in This Book

Start a personal plan on how you can personally bring more intentional contact into each of these cultures, especially with people you do not feel connected to already (expand your box!). Contact does not even need to include touch right away, or with everyone. It can mean eye contact paired with a smile. It can also mean a tap on the shoulder, a high-five, or a handshake with an arm touch. Contact + Connection = Compassionate feeling.

Third, Check In Frequently

Every day, ask the following: Did I have any connection with others? Was I present/aware? Did I give my full attention to my mom/ friend/ child? Remember, your touch and smile can create all the difference to them, while also bringing positive physical and mental benefits to yourself.

Fourth, Start a Conversation

Begin a simple conversation with someone you know, regardless of their age, about social isolation and loneliness. Identify opportunities to offer touch to those people. Who do you know whose children are heading to college? Who lost a significant other through death or a break-up? Have you met someone at work or social event coming from a new place? How can you invite them in and make them feel welcome, even if you just start with a smile, eye-gaze, and handshake? (Remember: Social isolation is subjective whereas loneliness is objective. One can be socially isolated and not lonely, or lonely while around people.)

Finally, Start a Conversation with the Child/ren in Your Life

Spark a conversation with your child/grandchild/cousin/etc. about touch and what they like and do not like. Start honoring their touch needs/wants. Empower them to speak up about what they want with you and others they trust so they can speak up when it becomes outside of their comfort zone or when they need something beyond what they are getting. Once that is comfortable for them, encourage them to do the same with others. These communication skills will build confidence and will be applicable in many different aspects of their lives.

One conversation, one eye-gaze and smile, or one consensual touch will ignite the possibilities for more connection and collaboration in our culture.

It's what we need most, and it is up to us to start the revolution to solve *The Touch Crisis*.

"People will forget what you said,
people will forget what you did,
but people will never forget
how you made them feel."

~ Maya Angelou, American poet ~

CONCLUSION
OUR PATH FORWARD

As I walked down the jetway in the Stockholm airport for my journey home, my thoughts turned to what life would probably feel like upon my return to the U.S.

I cannot wait until I get back into my practice and can share all my new tools. The classes I took in Europe were amazing!

The last weeks had been a lovely distraction as I said "goodbye" to everyone.

So many lovely shared hugs—I have so much gratitude for all the people I've met.

I looked at the people around me as we boarded the plane, feeling curious about how they interacted with touch and what I could learn from each of them if I had time the way I had learned from people in hostels, on buses, and on trails.

Those I couldn't engage with taught me how easy it is to get accustomed to touch AND the absence of it. I'm so glad my re-entry will be so different than last time! The clarity I have now with strangers and friends to reach out and use my tools is exponential.

Smiling to myself and feeling empowered, I found my seat and tucked my case in the space in front of me, keeping my schedule and laptop out for the flight.

I know what to expect with touch sensitivity this time and have new skills to navigate it. Plus, I am committed to communicating clear requests for touch, while being curious instead of fearful if I get upsetting reactions.

I opened my calendar to review my initial plan for speaking, workshops, and retreats in 2020.

It's going to be so incredible to build a community and create spaces that help people bring awareness to themselves and their own touch terrain. Talk about a powerful way to tune into themselves and practice intentional touch communication in a safe environment, as well as learn new ways to heal their bodies.

I felt the excitement rise again as I pictured the cozy, safe, retreat houses I had found. Especially the day-retreats, where people could explore natural settings as they explored themselves.

We can all learn from tuning in and sharing with each other. It's powerful to know that others have similar fears, hesitations, and successes.

Closing my eyes, I could see the faces of clients who had improved their own physical, mental, and emotional health over the years. I had seen them recover from challenges from knee pain and swelling; to shoulder problems that had not responded to traditional medical treatments; to fears and panic attacks. Once we brought awareness to their body sensations and started troubleshooting and giving them resources so they could empower themselves to take action in their own lives and heal, the results were amazing.

And the potential is only amplified now. I only wish I could share their incredible stories. I think others would be amazed at what they can change in themselves—even things that are supposedly genetic or "un-fixable." It's not easy, but it is so worth the journey.

My mind went through some of the more challenging personal healing journeys I had navigated over the last twenty years of healing.

Goodness knows I've done a lot more healing over the last few months while I could tune in. Tapping while I was on trails, self-exploration and journaling on busses, and quiet time to sit and reflect on my communication with people and how I can make it better. Stirring up emotionally-charged things from the past as I wrote, then looking at them from a new perspective and an open mind. Plus, I've navigated the cultural terrain in a variety of countries, while also preparing myself for the culture shock when I return home such a different person.

As the safety demonstration started, I tuned into all the physical changes in my body and improvement of symptoms I had taken to Europe with me.

The internal wisdom is so powerful when we learn to listen. EFT, CranioSacral, and classical homeopathy are so dynamic and can clear so many old beliefs and patterns.

I had done a lot more than that to heal, but those were my three main touchstones.

(Ha, touchstones.)

I focused on my breath as the plane sped up for takeoff, excited to return to my community a healthier, happier version of me.

It's going to take all of us and our teams to heal *The Touch Crisis*. We need to remember and recognize the scientific importance of touch to our physical, emotional, and mental well-being not only as individuals, but as a culture as a whole. As we awaken our child-like nature, become curious, and question touch fears and restrictions, we can harness self-knowledge to address unresolved issues in our past. We can mobilize our own healing power, as well as find professionals to help facilitate our healing through a safe environment and neural regulation.

Once we feel safe we can begin to create and implement our intentions to ask for what we need. If asking for touch at first seems too intimidating, we can begin asking for what we need in small ways such as asking for a blanket at our massage therapist's office, an extra side of dressing at a restaurant, help with the laundry, or a hand with something heavy. We can say *no* to a request that does not align with our needs. We can move into creating safe, intentional touch and communication with our families and friends. As we identify our wants and needs and understand consent, we can greet others with compassion and a helpful attitude if they have not learned these skills yet. We can be gracious and withhold judgment and assumptions, and understand that not everyone will see eye-to eye.

Let me be clear: we will *not* always see eye-to-eye. I was reminded of this when a healer reached out to me on LinkedIn. As we chatted about his new machine that helped people heal and I explained I was in Europe and writing this book, he stated, "Soap Box Time: I'[m] a proponent of no touch... Consensual touch...how about consensual energy too? Like, if people in the US are going to be arrogant and intrusive, can they just not leave their own spaces and effect [sic] other people's energy?"

I could have taken this as an attack, taken it personally, judged him for being a healer while seemingly lacking compassion, or challenged him on finding his own energy regulation and protection methods. However, I chose to reply that I respected his decision. I shared my point of view as simply and succinctly as I could, without being attached to the outcome or trying to change his mind. Then I used it as an opportunity to learn how to speak about what we are doing differently to help even more people. I even thought about reaching out again to get more of his opinion on why he believed in no-touch, but chose not to—yet. Learning to take responsibility only for our own level of communication, trying to be as clear as we can, and finding compassion for others will help us succeed in our journey to embrace safe and consensual touch in our communities. We start with ourselves, then with our families and friends, and then with acquaintances, subcultures, and perhaps even would-be strangers.

The key is to stay committed to ourselves and our own desires, and to see the larger positive impact we can have in our communities. Instead of focusing on small (or large) setbacks, we can share in the joy expressed by people who have a positive impact from our efforts. Personally, I know publishing this book will open me up to confrontations of all sorts, and I am not sure when and how they will manifest themselves. However, I feel strongly about my decision, and I have a strong system of friendships for support and healers for the more complicated or personal issues that may emerge. The key for all of us is to actually ask for help when we need it instead of trying to manage all the emotions, challenges, and hurdles by ourselves. Any worthwhile journey will have some rocky terrain; and we can learn from our successes, too.

Learning about ourselves and strategizing our own comfort in approaching consensual touch is just the beginning—the first layer of change and healing. As we take action we will find ourselves facing triggers and challenges that require some support from someone who has been there/done that and has the tools to help us more deeply embody the framework in a way that makes it easier to bring out into the community. The invitation is for you to consider going to retreats where there are opportunities to learn more about touch and practice your skills. Bring someone that can be your partner and cohort in the changes you want to see and that you envision for your community. *The Touch Crisis* in our culture needs us to step up and be brave, while also being cautious and mindful as we take risks and make mistakes.

Do you think that having deeply satisfying relationships, a physical body that is healthy and nurtured with plenty of cuddling hormone (oxytocin) and less stress hormone (cortisol), and a regulated and calm nervous system for ourselves and our loved ones is worth it? Do you agree that decreasing cultural violence and communication and trust challenges is worth taking small, measured steps to improve? I strongly believe the benefits outweigh any risks and the discomfort we are likely to face while taking the journey.

As we learn and grow, and as we let our inner light shine (instead of being ruled by fear), we will bring other people up as well. We can help them use touch to find their own emotional balance and feel they belong. We can empower others so they are comfortable speaking up for their own wants and needs throughout their lives so they can avoid some of the same turmoil we have experienced. We can use touch to help regulate the brains of our youth, so they are less likely to commit violence or to turn to damaging relationships just to feel important and connected. As we master and teach safety in touch, we will expand the skills in our larger group communities and workplaces.

Imagine for a moment being in a community where women and men alike can communicate clearly around their touch boundaries, without it having to be a burden. Where it is as easy as saying "hello" or "great weather today." Where touch is not automatically assumed to be sexual or controlling. Where people feel good both giving and receiving high-fives or pats on the shoulder or handshakes, and it revitalizes them. Where you feel the freedom in your own body as you realize that your *yes* and *no* will be honored and respected as you start surrounding yourself with people who also dream of and envision healthy communities.

This can be reality. I know it because I have experienced communities and groups that function in alignment with these principles. I have created friendships with both men and women that embody these principles.

So let's band together, pack our bags, and set out on the trail to make this vision a reality.

THE STATISTICS IN THE TIME OF COVID

In late 2019, even before the culture was in upheaval over COVID, Cigna was observing how daily interactions with others were key indicators of loneliness. With 80 being the highest possible 'lonely' score, they note, "those who interact with people daily have an average loneliness score of 41.1, nearly 20 points lower than those who never interact with other people (60.4)."

What's at stake here now? Touch has become highly politicized as we morally and ethically explore our own beliefs around suggested and forced no-touch policies and make our own health decisions. Many statistics in this book, about the damage caused by lack-of-touch and non-healthy touch, are now becoming outdated (and updated) as we hear reports about increased violence in homes and in society, skyrocketing depression and suicide rates, loneliness, and even death from loneliness occurring as communities and families have not been permitted to physically interact.

JAMA (Journal of the American Medical Association) Psychiatry was one of the many places to talk about downfalls of physical distancing outside of the home. "Secondary consequences of social distancing may increase the risk of suicide,"[75] they said, citing economic stress, social isolation, national anxiety, and decreased access to spiritual and community support as some of the risk factors.

"A broad body of research links social isolation and loneliness to poor mental health; and recent data shows that significantly higher shares of people who were sheltering in place (47%) reported negative mental health effects resulting from worry or stress related to coronavirus than among those not sheltering in place (37%)."[76]

Not only is the isolation damaging mentally and emotionally, it has physical consequences as well. Physically, "social distancing by staying home can lead to a decline in positive health behaviors, including diet, sleep and exercise,"[77] according to California State University, Fullerton. The National Institute of Health has articles reporting the dramatic consequence for those who cannot hide from non-healthy touch. "While actions such as encouraging individuals to adopt 'social distancing,' mandating school and business closures, and imposing travel restrictions may reduce the transmission of the infectious disease, unfortunately not all are finding safety in the resulting seclusion. Many family violence (domestic violence, child abuse, and pet abuse) victims may currently be facing a "worst case" scenario — finding themselves trapped in the home with a violent perpetrator during a time of severely limited contact with the outside world."[78]

While suicide and depression rates DECREASED after the events of 9/11/2001 because of the sense of community created by the mutual loss, we are watching our communities being pulled apart and isolated as we are encouraged to look down on, judge, or shame each other for not wearing masks (or for wearing them) or for giving a hug outside of our circle. I encourage us all to take a step back, open up, and consider the long-term impact of shaming others and refusing to engage in healthy touch. We can create a sense of community again when we use our tools of compassion, empathy, communication, and (as much as we can) healthy touch.

ABOUT DAWN BENNETT

Dawn Bennett, Founder of Touch Remedies, has a multitude of alternative and complementary health care practice certifications, in addition to her BA in Business and Complementary Medicine. She loves empowering small groups, individuals, and large audiences to embrace powerful new ways to transform themselves and their communities with her unique blend of empathy, humor, and just enough attitude to challenge social norms.

Dawn's background as a Massage and CranioSacral Therapist, homeopath, Emotional Freedom Techniques Practitioner, and student of all modalities that help individuals and communities heal, combined with her experience of speaking, teaching college-level massage for more than ten years, building an award-winning massage business from scratch, and traveling across the world, has inspired and equipped her to become a leader ready and willing to address the touch crisis in our culture. Having grown up in an era when it was okay to give hugs to teachers and when warnings about touch were only about getting into trouble sexually, she was upset when the experience of touch shifted from acceptable to confusing, awkward, and even dangerous in schools and workplace cultures. Eventually, Dawn immersed herself in the science of touch and quickly discovered an important new factor in the terrifying increases in anxiety, depression, and addiction that we are seeing in America.

Committed to leading the tough conversations and walking alongside those who want to join the healing touch revolution, she works with people individually, in groups, and in intimate retreat settings. With her support, clients begin to mend their own histories and challenges, speak their needs, and acquire the tools they need to say *yes* and *no* and enjoy the real benefits of healthy touch in every arena of their lives.

Today she has hundreds of clients who, she is proud to say, have done their own deep work and restored their inner power and potential, released physical and emotional symptoms and struggles, and found their own potential and voice in their work, relationships, and volunteer communities.

Dawn founded, owned, and sold a business that won "Service Business of the Year" two years in a row. She has been called a "zen hummingbird" because of her propensity to be chill, introspective, and in-tune; and then suddenly embrace her inner child, explode with energy and movement, and get an obnoxious amount of stuff done in a very short amount of time. She loves to travel and enjoy the healing powers of nature. She also loves people dearly and is working on saying so more often.

A SPECIAL INVITATION FROM DAWN

This book was written to encourage people to embrace touch as another method for connecting and healing oneself and the communities that surround us.

If you have been challenged and/or inspired by this book to reach deeper within and take touch to the next level in your own life and in the lives of those who surround you, you do not have to do it alone.

If you need or want more support,
or want to hire Dawn to inspire
your audience, please go to:

www.TouchRemedies.com

Get 50% Off Your First Level 1 Class!
Discount Code: TOUCHCRISIS

Go to www.TouchRemedies.com today for the latest classes, specials, and opportunities.

EXTRA RESOURCES

When the feelings become distracting, I invite you to pause and take care of yourself in one or more of the following ways.

First, take care of yourself by setting your intention and creating your own sense of safety. I invite you to breathe, feel your feet on the floor or your bum on your chair, and explore for yourself what is coming up for you. Many find writing or journaling helpful. Maybe a walk is more your style. Maybe you need to shout in frustration or fear or anger. Perhaps reaching out to someone else and talking it through is best for you. Be clear that whatever you choose to do to help yourself is working toward your understanding of self and healing, not preventing it. What makes you feel centered, calm, and alive? That may be the best way to move the energy and emotions through you and allow yourself to re-center instead of shutting yourself down or forcing your way stubbornly through a challenge.

Second, approach this new conversation the way a child would learn a new topic. Be playful with these ideas.

Take a child-like curiosity about how you can integrate these concepts, tools, and suggestions into your life and your community in a way that feels good for you—while honoring others' wishes and boundaries. We all have our own backgrounds culturally and socially; and we have stories and life experiences that influence the way we perceive, give, and receive physical contact. Look at which crossroad you wish to take and try to shift "negative" responses into compassionate ones that assume we are all doing our best at any moment in time. If you feel triggered by another, assume it is not intended and ask questions, create a boundary, or speak your truth. If you find an emotion turning toward self-criticism or judgment, do the same for yourself. Give yourself and others grace and time to absorb and integrate the changes you wish to see and apply. Play. Smile. Explore.

Third, find someone to talk to. For some it might be enough to join the Touch Remedies online group, but I realize that others are coming to the conversation with bigger touch traumas, challenges, and stories. If that's you, please join us and also rally a support system around you and include some combination of professionals such as a therapist, counselor, Emotional Freedom Techniques (tapping) Practitioner, body worker, coach, homeopath, healer, etc. for maximum support and results.

Fourth, focus on personal healing before you try to take this to a system, community, or culture. When challenges arise outside of you, look into yourself and identify the sensation and emotion. What old pattern or social or childhood training is asking to be addressed? Observe and honor changes in yourself and others. You'll know when the people around you are ready to hear from you about this when they mention that you have changed in some way or express curiosity about what is creating the change. In the meantime, share your suggestions, successes, challenges, inquiries, and questions with your inner circle and our online community.

Always remember, we can change our communities through healthy touch and boundaries without drama. We can choose to participate in a process where we connect with others and teach other generations to embrace touch in a way that feels good for everyone. We can smile and giggle and encourage curiosity and wonder and play. We can cuddle and hug and touch in non-sexual ways to ease our loneliness and give our brain what it needs and deserves. It's a process. It's an ever-changing and shifting concept.

Resources for Help

U.S. National Suicide Prevention Lifeline
1-800-273-8255

Rape, Abuse, and Incest National Network (RAINN)
1-800-656-4673
www.rainn.org/

National Domestic Violence Hotline
1-800-799-7233
www.thehotline.org/help/

Love is Respect – National Teen Dating Abuse Hotline
1-866-331-9474
Text: 22522
www.loveisrespect.org/

ChildHelp National Child Abuse Hotline
1-800-422-4453
www.childhelp.org/

CLIMB HIGHER
THE PLAY & EXPLORE WORKBOOK

Play and Explore

Chapter 1
Ruts & Remedies
Scouting Your Inner Terrain

Most of us need more touch, and the science shows us why. The challenge is that, like me before the Hoffman Process and the "shaming incident," most of us don't really take the time to think about our experience with touch. We operate on those patterns that have been conditioned, and we are rarely forced to evaluate them.

So, let's do that now.

Answer the following questions and, as you do, notice your emotional and physical reactions. Name any emotions you are feeling (i.e. shame, grief, joy, fear, sadness, disgust, amusement.) Be playful and curious with your self-investigation. This is about exploring yourself so you can learn, not comparing or judging.

Remember, take care of yourself how you need and when you need! Give yourself freedom to take a break, breathe, get angry, get sad, or reach out to someone in your support circle or the Touch Remedies group. This is about you and your learning and growth process, so be gentle with yourself as well as your life experiences.

In Public

1. How do you feel watching intimate touch on a movie screen? In real life? Does it change if you are around kids or family?
2. How do you feel in a crowd when people are naturally touching you?
3. What is your visceral response to a woman not wanting to help a child in need on the playground?
4. How would you feel at a park if a couple was being really touchy? Is that different if you are on public transportation? In a nice restaurant?
5. What is the "right kind of touch" for public? How far is too far? (Between friends, family, partners, etc.)

At Work

1. What are the written and unwritten rules around touch in your working environment?
2. How do those serve the environment?

3. How do those hurt the environment?
4. How would you like to express touch in your work environment?
5. If people are on equal levels in the organization (no power dynamics involved), do you think consensual touch should be allowed? Why or why not?

Friend & Partnership Touch

Answer these questions twice. Once for your good/close friends in general, and once for your ideal partner.

1. How do you touch each other? (Where on the body? How often? How intentionally? How is it reciprocated or not?
2. How would you like to touch and be touched?
3. Is that desire met?
4. What would need to change for you to give and receive what you want and need?
5. How do you currently communicate your touch needs and aversions?

Touch with Children

1. How do you touch children in the community? (Your friends' children, your child's friends, a lost child looking for his/her parents, etc.)
2. How do you touch your children? (Think about how often, how intentionally, and how it is received by them.)

3. How do your children touch you? (Think about how often, how intentionally, and how it is received by you.)
4. Would you like more or less? Why?
5. What makes it currently dissatisfactory for you?

Family of Origin

1. What was touch like in your family? Was it attentive? Lacking? Abusive? A reward?
2. What were the beliefs around touching others? Who was "okay" to touch and who was not? Was that based upon relationship, culture, closeness, values, etc?
3. Were you forced to give and/or receive hugs or touch when you didn't want to, including friends, family members, or other people in your community?
4. What were you taught about the relationship between touch and sex?
5. Where do your beliefs and desires around touch not resonate with your family of origin or your upbringing?

Beginning to Understand Your Inner Terrain and Personal Touch Boundaries

Body-Emotion Awareness & Knowledge

1. What emotions came up while you were answering the questions?

2. How did you perceive the 'positive" versus "negative" emotions in your body?
3. Look at the similarities and differences between your answers in the various sections. What about touch is comfortable and uncomfortable for you? Why do you think that is?
4. How do your beliefs/actions impact your interaction with touch (ex: keep you safe, prevent you from keeping boundaries, inspire fear, restrict or enhance your ability to ask for what you want/need, etc.)?

Root Understanding
Explore the roots of your answers. Are your beliefs, feelings, reactions and understandings cultural? Social? Religious? Experiential? From childhood? Adulthood? Are your answers different depending on who is initiating the touch? Are there any arenas in which you were surprised by your reaction?

Deeper Contemplation
Go back to each of the above environments and identify one or two people from each culture/situation that you are familiar with.
1. What does it feel like when you think about reaching out and touching that person on the arm or giving them a hug? Where does that reaction come from?
2. What does it feel like when you think about that person touching you on the arm or giving you a hug? Where does that reaction come from?

3. Is there a dissonance between the two answers? If so, why?
4. Considering individuals in any culture, does the age of the person matter? If so, what is the upper and lower limit? Does gender matter?
5. What patterns around touch were created for you that no longer suit you?

Play and Explore

Chapter 2
Routes and Resources
Strategizing Your Intention and Safety

As a reminder, safety is experienced on a spectrum, rather than just existing or not. We experience it in physical, mental, and emotional spheres, and we often use our conditioning, observations, and gut feelings to determine where on the spectrum we are—from life-threatening danger to complete safety.

The point is, safety is not static. It is subject to change based on a multitude of factors. These exercises are intended to help you find your own sense of intention and safety around touch. After all, the more we understand what we enjoy and what makes us feel safe in our own world, we have an easier time finding boundaries and communicating to others.

Exercises to Develop Your Safety and Intention

Exercise 1: Self-hugs

Hug yourself. Right now. Wrap your arms around yourself, and hold them there. How does that feel to give yourself comfort and touch? How can you sink into it and make it feel better for you? If you relax your shoulders, allow your arms to soften, sit in a different position—how can this moment of self-care and self-love nurture you?

If you resist giving yourself a hug, why? Some people have learned it's wrong to love and nurture self. Or that it's weak to nurture oneself. Perhaps there's an underlying sense that we don't deserve to love ourselves, or that love comes only from the outside.

We must be able to respect and care for, even love ourselves before we can truly accept care and love from others. If we don't appreciate ourselves, outside affection will only be a band-aid, temporary relief, for what we need as humans, including a sense of belonging. Self-love is a lifelong process for some, but taking the first steps, at least to self-respect and acceptance, can bring us a long way in creating safety for ourselves in the world.

Exercise 2: Inanimate Objects

Grab an inanimate object nearby that you can hold in your hand, preferably one with multiple textures or surfaces (i.e. a pencil, a rock, a calculator, your watch, etc.). Get relaxed and comfortable, close your eyes, and really feel the object in your hand. Notice its temperature, texture, weight. How does it feel when you touch it? Notice the sensations in your hands and in your body. Do you feel more safe or comfortable using one object over another? For example, does working with something soft or hard, or something light or heavy, create more of a sensation of safety or comfort for you?

Can you tune into the sensations of the clothes you are wearing? What does the fabric feel like on your skin? Is it rough, soft, tight, tickling, or comforting?

Now play with feeling something larger. Perhaps an object you can cuddle with, put on your lap, or wrap around you. Ideas include a stone, a book, a blanket, a pillow, a warm cup of tea, or a laptop case. Can you really tune into the sensation in your body as it contacts this object?

Exercise 3: Animals

For many people animals are a great transition into the world of touch. If you are not ready to expand your touch with people (or even if you are), start by finding an animal you can touch, whether it be a dog, cat, or bird. If you don't have one, connect with a friend's pet or find a nearby shelter and find an animal you would like to interact with. Often you can take them into rooms or take them for walks. Not only can it be great for the animals who are lacking in touch, but it is a safer way for you to have time to be in tune with your own needs, explore your quality of touch, and to play with different intentions of touch.

Most domestic pets, unless they have a history of abuse or have been trained to tolerate more than they desire, are also masters of consent. No matter what kind of unconditional love they have for you, if they don't want you to touch them, they will stay out of reach. If you aren't touching them attentively or as they desire, they will either nudge you to get your attention, start moving around to help you find "the spot," or just get up and leave.

Once you have your animal with you, observe him/her, as well as how you feel in your own body. When you are clear, move yourself in to a position where you can interact with and touch him/her. Some animals may not give you time to tune in, and will instead bombard you with a demand for attention, but feel into that as well. What is it like for you in your mind and body when the animal demands a certain type of touch from you? What feels safe for you? What positions or interactions with the animal feel better for both you and the animal? For example, if you were to put your face in its face, would that feel okay for you and the animal?

If the animal doesn't want touch, you get to practice honoring that the animal is doing what it needs for itself in that moment. Maybe it is scared, tired, hungry, overstimulated, or lonely. Maybe it hasn't had a lot of touch and doesn't know what to make of it yet. Maybe it has some trust issues. Be patient and observe your own internal sensations and feelings, as well as what your brain is telling you. This alone can teach you a lot about your own fears, concerns, self-judgments, and patterns of being. Do these feelings and sensations resonate with other situations in the past?

The level of awareness you build through these exercises will help you begin to find your own sense of safety and begin setting intentions for more healthy touch in your life.

Play and Explore

Chapter 3
Crossroads and Choices
Tackling the Mountain of Wants,
Needs, and Consent

In chapter one I invited you to look at touch roots, emotions, and boundaries in a few different categories. If you took the time to answer those, hopefully your deeper knowledge about yourself has been informing and waking up your own wants, needs, and boundaries. In chapter two I asked you to start waking up your touch awareness using inanimate objects and animals and feeling into a sense of safety for yourself and them. In this chapter we are exploring your own pleasure and your wants and needs.

Exercise 1: Inanimate Objects
Go back to the second exercise in chapter two with the inanimate object. But this time, beyond just sensing the physical attributes, see if you can find pleasure in your hands by touching it. In other words, instead of using your hands to feel it, use IT to touch YOU—your hand, fingertips, the back of your hands, perhaps your wrists or your legs. How does it feel? Can you find a way to receive enjoyment from the object? Try smiling and breathing. Stay playful and open. The more relaxed you are and the slower and lighter you move the object against your skin, the easier this exercise will be. The goal is to open yourself to finding enjoyment through your sensory nerves. Wake up your hands to the possibility of *enjoying* the input of touch, rather than just processing it. You can practice this exercise anytime, anywhere, to condition your hands to become more sensitive and to train yourself to experience pleasure from the smallest amount of intentional, safe touch.

You may repeat this exercise using your own skin-to-skin contact. Be really intentional with the way you contact yourself and do it with respect, care, and curiosity. What is it like to use your hand to feel your face? Your arm? Play with increasing your awareness on both the "giving" and "receiving" side.

Exercise 2: Animals
Go back to the third exercise in chapter two with the animal. Find the same or another animal and repeat the process. But this time, include an additional focus. Remember the exercise you did with the inanimate object? Explore in a similar intention with this animal. Next, bring an intention of touching it for your own pleasure and really experiencing in your own hands the texture of fur, feathers, nose, tail, feet, or wherever you merge in touch. What is it like to touch to *give* it pleasure, and what is it like to touch to *receive* pleasure? What do you want and need, and what can you sense that the animal wants or needs? How can you honor that? How does the animal give consent or take it away?

Exercise 3: Strategy
I would like to invite you to start playing with the idea of increasing the amount, quality, or type of touch with three people you are close to in a way that is consensual for both of you. Tune into your wants and needs, and find a way to ask that sounds genuine to you while holding the integrity of your own boundaries. Think about ways in which you can make requests you are sure will be granted if this idea scares you.

Amount = Number of touches per day/week. Can you give this person one extra touch, hug, high-five, etc.?

Quality = This refers to setting a strong intention to communicate positive emotion through your touch with them. Instead of giving your friend a quick hello hug, can you really try to infuse all of your love and respect for him/her into your touch?

Type = If you usually give a handshake, but have wanted to hug this person, will you ask for one? How about shifting from a handshake to a handshake with a touch on the arm? How about from no touch to a high-five?

Stage 1

1. Name three people you feel safe enough to touch or to start touching in a different way.

2. Write down how you would like to change the touch with them.

3. Write down a few notes about what you might say (more on this in the next chapter) to this person as you share your wants and needs.

4. Look at ways that you might subconsciously create a block to that happening (avoiding, body language, unaddressed emotions, allowing old habits, etc.).

5. Leave a column or space to fill out at the end of chapter four.

Your example could look something like this:

Name	Touch Change	Communication	Potential block/s
My roommate Jess	Add one hug a day	Tell her I'm playing with adding more touch into my life and ask if she would like a hug when she gets home from work. (We gave each other hugs all the time before we lived together.)	Being too busy when she comes home or overwhelming her when she does get home
The massage therapist at work	Add a hug when we see each other	Tell her that I always want to hug her when I see her because I think she's so amazing, but I didn't know how to ask before. Is that something she would like, or would she prefer to keep it as it is?	Telling myself she's too busy. Fear of rejection. Making sure I'm not in the same space as her on Thursday.
Dad	More intentional hugs	I will hug him with more intention.	Falling into old habit and not being present when hugging. Allowing a hug before I've set everything down when I walk in the door instead of asking him to wait a second.

Note that when I am asking for increase of touch, I am asking if it is something *they also want*. I am not just asking if they will do it for me. This clarity in asking can help keep the give/receive balance more equal. If we both want it, there is equality. If they are doing it *for* me, then perhaps we should negotiate something different. You can also communicate to your people that just because you are both trying something new, you would appreciate feedback if their desire changes at any time—to increase or to back off with touch. This way, you can play with different consent experiences.

Before starting these conversations, I recommend you read chapter four for additional tools and ideas.

Stage 2
Play with the concept of approaching the conversation of touch in each of the following cultures in a way that feels comfortable to you. Just because you write it here doesn't mean you actually have to take action on it tomorrow; but use this exercise as a way to honor and validate your own needs, as well as to begin to find words that can help you move gently toward the type of touch you want in all areas of your life. The conversations don't have to be asking for touch, but can be establishing a base boundary of touch in the future. As a reminder, the cultures/communities I had you evaluate were: public, work, friend/partnership, children, family of origin.

Please make your own categories that fit you. Public may turn into a few different categories of spiritual community, volunteer organization events, or acquaintances. Friend and partnership may get split into two. Children may need to split, as teenage boys will require different communication than your twenty-five-year-old daughter or your six-year-old son.

Take note. Are you feeling resistance around going through with this? Take a few deep breaths. Use the self-awareness in this phase of your own healing work, and play with overcoming the resistance. Add those to any potential body language, time, or habitual blocks that may come up as well, for your own awareness. I added a few examples below. I also added a column for you to play with the idea of when might be a good time to approach them after reading chapter four. Just like my example with my former husband, think of a situation that would be fitting for both of you.

Public	Touch	Ask	Potential block/s
My son's best friend's mom	Celebratory high-fives	We are always watching the boys play football together, and when they make a big play, I want to give someone a high-five. I feel close enough to you to ask what your touch boundaries are and if that is something you are comfortable with. What would you like?	I don't feel like she accepts me.

Amy, the head of the annual fundraiser	Hug	I honor all the work you are doing for this fundraiser, and sometimes it looks like you are overwhelmed and just need a hug. I don't know your boundaries, but want you to know that if you need a pat on the shoulder or a hug to help you ground, just ask. I'm really open to touch.	She might see me as unprofessional or take it wrong. I might find tasks to do to avoid talking to her about it.

Work People	Touch	Ask	Potential block/s
Cindy the receptionist	Touching her arm	I often touch my friend's arm when I am talking to emphasize a point or to feel connected. I talk with you often on our way out of the building at night, and want to respect your boundaries and our working environment. Is that something that feels comfortable for you?	I've had closed body language with her and might do it again.
Kathy, partner in the merger project	Hug	Every time we make a big success, I get so excited I want to hug you, but I have no idea what your touch boundaries are, especially since we work together. What is your view on touch at work?	I haven't expressed anything before with her, so this might be too big of a step.

Family	Touch	Ask	Potential block/s
My husband	Hug before bedtime	We have gotten into the habit of just saying good night and wandering off to bed whenever we are tired. Can we start making an effort to give a good hug before bed?	Kids get in the way. I have to get stuff ready for work the next day. I might get too involved in the tv program. He might laugh at me.
My fourteen-year-old daughter	Hug	I want to respect your touch boundaries and your need or lack of desire for touch. I realized I would like more touch from you. Are you open to trying to add one hug in a day? I'll let you lead and do it when it feels right for you.	She'll be on her phone and I won't want to interrupt her. I'll be on my phone.
My sixteen-year-old son	High-five	I know you are at an age where you may not want to give me hugs right now, but I really appreciate the validation I feel when you make an effort to connect. Would you consider giving me a hug or at least a high-five to say hello when you come through the door? I'll let you lead so you don't feel embarrassed if your friends are around.	I am afraid I won't say the right words.

Tune in. How did it feel to write this list? How are you feeling in your body? Congratulate yourself!

I applaud you for taking the first steps to really honor what you want and need, as well as bring your awareness and focus to a plan. It can be hard to ask for what you want, so remember to celebrate every success of your journey, no matter how small it seems.

Now, let's gather a few more tools before we have these conversations!

Play and Explore

Chapter 4
Yodels & Poles
Scaling the Challenges with the 4 C's

In chapter four we explored ways to be compassionate, curious, and communicative. Commitment is the key to creating lasting changes. One way to embrace a high level of communication is to script or plan for ways to say *no*, the same way we played with scripts and ways to asked for touch in chapter three. Saying *no*, as well as knowing your go-to supports and resources, is an important part of self-care.

Communication

Exercise 1

Make a list of ways to say *no* to an action but *yes* to you for each category: public, work, friend/partner, children, family of origin. Some of these can be the same no matter who you are talking to. Remember, you do not have to justify or explain why as a self-defense, but you can redirect or offer another option to say *yes* to the person. Even though your examples may include that, the most powerful *no* is *no, no thank you,* or something similar. Saying *not now* leaves a sense of ambiguity. If not now, when? So try to be clearer for yourself and for them. Use words that feel resonant and genuine for you.

Examples include the following:

Public

- No, but thank you for the offer.
- Oh, thanks for the hug offer, but I'd rather shake your hand.
- Thank you for showing your concern by touching my shoulder, but I feel better when people just listen.

Work

- Thank you for that, but I prefer to touch only through handshakes at work.
- I am glad you want to connect. Some days I am not up for touch, so I would love it if you asked before touching me.

Friend/ Partner/ Family of Origin

- I'm not up for a hug right now, but I really want to know how your day was.

- I'm all touched out today, but I'd love to go for a walk/sit on the couch/raincheck for tomorrow.
- I feel like I've given all day at work. I would love to spend time with you, but I need twenty minutes for myself first.
- I am trying to create new touch boundaries for myself, so since you are family, I am going to practice with you.

Children (this is all going to depend on age, personality, former boundaries, mood, etc.)

- Let's do some self-hug practice right now! You hug you and I'll hug me for a few seconds.
- You know how sometimes you need a bit of space and don't want your sister to touch you? I need a bit of space like that right now. How about we do that in five minutes?
- I would love to snuggle you now, but how about we do that after dinner when I can really spend time? How about a quick high-five to make our agreement?

Exercise 2

It's important to practice your *no* and *stop* before you have to use them—when you start enduring or you realize you do not want what is happening to continue. Think of one or two current situations or people that you would like to say *no* to. Create a couple phrases for each of them that can help you set boundaries *and* feel powerful, clear, and compassionate. These phrases can be used for touch situations and other situations where what you want and need is not being honored.

Examples include the following:

- Stop.
- Please stop.
- Please pause. I am feeling _____ and would like to tune in for a moment and see what I really need/what is comfortable for me.
- I don't like _____. I would prefer _____.
- Hold on, I need a minute or two.
- That is not feeling comfortable for me.
- I know that we do this often, but I feel I need more give-and-take. Can we set a time (later is often better if it is an emotionally charged situation) to see how we can both have what we want and need in this situation? (Note: Actually put it as a time/date and commit to it.)
- I want you to know that I value our connection, but I feel I need us to stop hugging at work. Would you be open to keeping it to just a handshake?
- Some days I am really energetically tapped. It would be so great for me if you could check in with me before touching me.
- I want our connection to be genuine. Will you stop touching me on the shoulder like that? I would really prefer _____.

Start using touch, communicating about touch, and be curious about others' needs. If someone hugs or touches you without asking for consent, commit to educating and redirecting with compassion—almost as a teacher would address a child who is learning—using a compassionate, playful, yet firm tone.

Extra Support for the Healing Journey

Exercise 3: Self-Care

A. In this process, emotions will emerge as well as old beliefs and patterns that may block you from expressing yourself. Identify ways you can emotionally care for yourself that feel self-nurturing, positive, and supportive. Try a gratitude walk—just walk around and start listing off aloud things you are grateful for—from the tiny things to the large things (i.e. I'm grateful that the sun is shining. I'm grateful that I had time to have an egg for breakfast. I'm grateful that I (or my partner or my children) have a job. I'm grateful that I don't have a job. I'm grateful that I have an amazing friend/partner. I'm grateful that I tried a new thing. I'm grateful that the birds are singing. I'm grateful that the birds are not singing. etc.). Perhaps for you, it feels more supportive and nurturing to journal, work out, scream into a pillow, take a few deep breaths or a tea break, or read positive affirmations about yourself. It may seem silly, but make a list right now. We can easily forget about simple tools (like deep breathing or journaling) when we are in the midst of strong emotion. Having a reminder resource somewhere where you see it regularly will help you remember to use your tools.

B. On that same list, write the names of friends that will support you as well—people you can call when you feel triggered. If you are anything like me, when I need support, I can forget to reach out to others, or my head can tell me reaching out is too weak, or I know that person "X" is at work and my mind says there is no one else to call. It's not true, so have that list ready and force yourself to call someone. Having a set schedule with a professional is also extremely helpful.

Completing Chapter Three's Grid

Exercise 4

Return to exercise three in chapter three; and if you haven't already started increasing the amount, quality, or type of touch with the three people you listed, now is the time. Fill out that last column and commit. Create a deadline or a goal to keep you accountable. For example, for my roommate Jess, I may decide to talk to her this Saturday morning (when we are both home and not stressed out). For the massage therapist at work, I may choose to talk to her at our mutual lunch break on Thursday.

Visualize how great it will be when you communicate with that person, and set your intention for a positive interaction between you.

Once that is done, work toward setting goals and deadlines for completing the second section that includes public, work, and family. Notice what comes up for you as you make those decisions; and find support to help you work through them, if needed. Remember, we would love to have you join our online Touch Remedies community where everyone is sharing their journey and finding support. Go to www.TouchRemedies.com to find the resource that suits you.

Play and Explore

Chapter 5
Campfires & Cookouts
Comparing Landscapes & Sharing the Adventure

Chapter five provided a variety of examples of ways that different subcultures interact with touch. Being curious and compassionate about similarities and differences can facilitate good communication and healthy touch practices between individuals.

Exercise 1
Make a list of the cultures (i.e. subcultures, communities, organizations, groups, workplaces, etc.) in which you engage. Don't get hung up on the categories—however

you want to label them is fine. This is just for bringing cultural clarity for yourself.

Who might you enlist to help you approach or create healthier touch in each of those cultures? What may need to change?

ENDNOTES

Introduction

1. Gopnik, Adam. "What the Science Of Touch Says About Us" *The New Yorker*, May 16, 2016, www.newyorker.com/magazine/2016/05/16/what-the-science-of-touch-says-about-us.
2. Field, Tiffany. *Touch*, second edition, Kindle, The MIT Press, 2014.
3. Field, Tiffany. *Touch*, second edition, Kindle, The MIT Press, 2014.
4. Light KC, Grewen KM, Amico JA. "More frequent partner hugs and higher oxytocin levels are linked to lower blood pressure and heart rate in premenopausal women." *Biol Psychol*. DOI: 10.1016/j.biopsycho.2004.11.002. 2005 Apr;69(1):5-21. Epub 2004 Dec 29.
5. Goleman, Daniel. "The Experience of Touch: Research Points to a Critical Role." *The New York Times*, Feb 2, 1988, www.nytimes.com/1988/02/02/science/the-experience-of-touch-research-points-to-a-critical-role.
6. Field, Tiffany. "Violence and touch deprivation in adolescents." *Adolescence*. 2002 Winter; 37(148):735-49. www.ncbi.nlm.nih.gov/pubmed/12564826

7. Youri R. Berends, Joke H. M. Tulen, André I. Wierdsma, Johannes van Pelt, Hjalmar J. C. van Marle. "Intranasal administration of oxytocin decreases task-related aggressive responses in healthy young males" *Psychoneuroendocrinology*. Volume 106. August 2019. Pages 147-154.

8. Hormone Health Network. "Oxytocin | Endocrine Society." *Hormone.org*. Endocrine Society, 10 March 2020. www.hormone.org/your-health-and-hormones/glands-and-hormones-a-to-z/hormones/oxytocin.

9. McLeod, Saul. "Maslow's Hierarchy of Needs." *Simply Psychology*. March 20, 2020, www.simplypsychology.org/maslow.html. Accessed May 2020

10. "Cigna U.S. Loneliness Index," 2018. www.multivu.com/players/English/8294451-cigna-us-loneliness-survey/docs/IndexReport_1524069371598-173525450.pdf

11. "Cigna U.S. Loneliness Index," 2018. www.multivu.com/players/English/8294451-cigna-us-loneliness-survey/docs/IndexReport_1524069371598-173525450.pdf

12. Stravynski A, Boyer R. "Loneliness in relation to suicide ideation and parasuicide: a population-wide study." *Suicide Life Threat Behav*. 2001 Spring;31(1):32-40. PMID:11326767 www.ncbi.nlm.nih.gov/pubmed/11326767. Accessed July 2019

13. Winerman, Lea. "By the numbers: An alarming rise in suicide." *American Psychological Association.* January 2019, Vol 50, No. 1. Print version: page 80. www.apa.org/monitor/2019/01/numbers. Accessed May 2020.

14. Criminal Justice Degree Hub.com. "Violent Crime: The US and Abroad," www.criminaljusticedegreehub.com/violent-crime-us-abroad/. Accessed October 2019.

15. Criminal Justice Degree Hub.com. "Violent Crime: The US and Abroad," www.criminaljusticedegreehub.com/violent-crime-us-abroad/. Accessed October 2019.

16. Gramlich, John. "What the data says about gun deaths in the U.S." *Pew Research Center*, August 16, 2019, www.pewresearch.org/fact-tank/2019/08/16/what-the-data-says-about-gun-deaths-in-the-u-s/, accessed November 2019.

17. James, Nathan. "Recent Violent Crime Trends in the United States." *Congressional Research Service*, June 20, 2018, fas.org/sgp/crs/misc/R45236.pdf, Accessed November 2019.

18. Lartey, Jamiles, Li, Weihua. "New FBI Data: Violent Crime Still Falling." *The Marshall Project,* September 30, 2019, www.themarshallproject.org/2019/09/30/new-fbi-data-violent-crime-still-falling. Accessed November 2019.

19. "Cigna U.S. Loneliness and The Workplace" January 2020. https://www.cigna.com/static/www-

cigna-com/docs/about-us/newsroom/studies-and-reports/combatting-loneliness/cigna-2020-loneliness-report.pdf. Accessed May 2020

20. Twenge, Jean M. "Have Smartphones Destroyed a Generation?" *The Atlantic,* September 2017, www.theatlantic.com/magazine/archive/2017/09/has-the-smartphone-destroyed-a-generation/534198/

21. "Cigna U.S. Loneliness and The Workplace" January 2020. https://www.cigna.com/static/www-cigna-com/docs/about-us/newsroom/studies-and-reports/combatting-loneliness/cigna-2020-loneliness-report.pdf. Accessed May 2020

Chapter 1

22. National Association for the Education of Young Children. "Prevention of Child Abuse in Early Childhood Programs and the Responsibility of Early Childhood Professionals to Prevent Child Abuse" 1996, pg 2. www.naeyc.org/sites/default/files/globally-shared/downloads/PDFs/resources/position-statements/PSCHAB98.PDF. Accessed November 2019

23. Borchard, Therese. "6 Benefits of Roughhousing for Kids." *Psych Central.* 2018, www.psychcentral.com/lib/6-benefits-of-roughhousing-for-kids/. Accessed July 2019

24. Floyd, Kory. (2014) "Relational and Health Correlates of Affection Deprivation." *Western*

Journal of Communication. 78:4, 383-403, DOI: 10.1080/10570314.2014.927071

25. Field, Tiffany. "Violence and touch deprivation in adolescents." *Adolescence.* 2002 Winter;37 (148):735-49. www.ncbi.nlm.nih.gov/pubmed/12564826. Accessed July 2019

26. Guéguen, Nicolas. "Nonverbal encouragement of participation in a course: the effect of touching." *Social Psychology of Education,* Kluwer Academic Publishers, 2004, www.communicationcache.com/uploads/1/0/8/8/10887248/effect_of_touch_on_encouragement_in_course_-_the_effect_of_touching_-_gueguen_2004.pdf. Accessed July 2019

27. Kraus, Michael & Huang, Cassey & Keltner, Dacher. "Tactile Communication, Cooperation, and Performance: An Ethological Study of the NBA." *Emotion* (Washington, D.C.). 2010. 10. 745-9. 10.1037/a0019382. Accessed June 2019

28. Mikolajczak M, Pinon N, Lane A, de Timary P, Luminet O. "Oxytocin not only increases trust when money is at stake, but also when confidential information is in the balance." Biol Psychol. 2010 Sep;85(1):182-4. doi: 10.1016/j.biopsycho.2010.05.010. Epub 2010 Jun 8. PMID: 20678992, www.ncbi.nlm.nih.gov/pubmed/20678992

29. Pepping GJ, Timmermans EJ. "Oxytocin and the biopsychology of performance in team sports." *ScientificWorldJournal.* 2012;2012:567363. Epub

2012 Sep 10. Review. www.ncbi.nlm.nih.gov/pubmed/22997498

30. van Ijzendoorn, Marinus H et al. "The Impact of Oxytocin Administration on Charitable Donating is Moderated by Experiences of Parental Love-Withdrawal." *Frontiers in Psychology.* vol. 2 258. 13 Oct. 2011, doi:10.3389/fpsyg.2011.00258. Accessed July 2019

31. Spechler, Diana. "The Power Of Touch: How Physical Contact Can Improve Your Health" *The Oprah Magazine.* December 6, 2017. www.huffpost.com/entry/the-power-of-touch-physical-contact-health_n_3253987.

32. Lipton, Bruce H, PhD. "Are You Programmed at Birth? How to transform the subconscious trance." August 17, 2010. www.healyourlife.com/are-you-programmed-at-birth

33. Goleman, Daniel. "The Experience of Touch: Research Points to a Critical Role" *New York Times.* February 2, 1988. www.nytimes.com/1988/02/02/science/the-experience-of-touch-research-points-to-a-critical-role.html?pagewanted=all

34. Chillot, Rick. "The Power of Touch" *Psychology Today.* March 2013, Rev. November 21, 2019. www.psychologytoday.com/gb/articles/201303/the-power-touch.

Chapter 2

35. *Beauty and the Beast.* Dir. Gary Trousdale, Kirk Wise. Walt Disney Pictures, 1991. Film.

36. Porges, Stephen W. "The polyvagal theory: new insights into adaptive reactions of the autonomic nervous system." *Cleveland Clinic Journal of Medicine* vol. 76 Suppl 2, 2009: S86-90. doi:10.3949/ccjm.76.s2.17

37. Williams, Lawrence E. Bargh, John A. "Experiencing Physical Warmth Promotes Interpersonal Warmth" *Science.* October 24, 2008. Vol 322. www.eduhk. hk/aclass/Resources/HE/staff/Wong%20 Wai%20Ho%20Savio/Williams_Science_cold_hot_ coffee_2009.pdf

38. Bargh, John. March 11, 2019. Blog Comment on "Now John Bargh's Famous Hot-Coffee Study has Failed to Replicate." January 2, 2019, https://digest.bps.org.uk/2019/01/02/now-john-barghs-famous-hot-coffee-study-has-failed-to-replicate/#comment-63119

39. Coan, Jim. "Why we hold hands." TedxCharlottesville, 2013. www.youtube.com/watch?v=1UMHUPPQ96c. Accessed June 2019

40. Hertenstein MJ, Holmes R, McCullough M, Keltner D. "The communication of emotion via touch." *Emotion.* 2009 Aug;9(4):566-73. doi: 10.1037/a0016108. PubMed PMID: 19653781. Accessed June 2019

41. Keltner, Dacher. "Hands On Research: The Science of Touch" *Greater Good Magazine. Education.* September 29, 2010. www.greatergood.berkeley.edu/article/item/hands_on_research. Accessed July 2019

42. "11 SCIENCE-BACKED TRUTHS ON THE POWER OF HUMAN TOUCH" *BrainFodder.* www.brainfodder.org/11-studies-human-touch/. Accessed June 2019

43. "Cigna U.S. Loneliness Index" 2018. www.multivu.com/players/English/8294451-cigna-us-loneliness-survey/docs/IndexReport_1524069371598-173525450.pdf

44. Holt-Lunstad J, Birmingham WA, Light KC. "Influence of a 'warm touch' support enhancement intervention among married couples on ambulatory blood pressure, oxytocin, alpha amylase, and cortisol." *Psychosomatic Med.* 2008 Nov;70(9):976-85. doi: 10.1097/PSY.0b013e318187aef7. Epub 2008 Oct 8. www.ncbi.nlm.nih.gov/pubmed/18842740. Accessed July 2019

45. Cohen, S., Janicki-Deverts, D., Turner, R. B., & Doyle, W. J. "Does Hugging Provide Stress-Buffering Social Support? A Study of Susceptibility to Upper Respiratory Infection and Illness." *Psychological Science,* 26(2), 135–147. 2015. doi.org/10.1177/0956797614559284. journals.sagepub.com/doi/10.1177/0956797614559284

46. Chillot, Rick. "The Power of Touch" *Psychology Today*. March 2013, Rev. November 21, 2019. www.psychologytoday.com/gb/articles/201303/the-power-touch

Chapter 3

47. "What is EFT Tapping?" *EFT International*. Par 2. eftinternational.org/discover-eft-tapping/what-is-eft-tapping/. Accessed May 2020

48. Keltner, Dacher. "Hands On Research: The Science of Touch." Greater Good Magazine. September 29, 2010, https://greatergood.berkeley.edu/article/item/hands_on_research. Accessed July, 2019.

49. "35 percent of British adults sleep with bear." Odd News, February 21, 2012, www.upi.com/Odd_News/2012/02/21/35-percent-of-British-adults-sleep-with-bear/49791329806031/?ur3=1.

50. Williams KD, Cheung CK, Choi W. "Cyberostracism: effects of being ignored over the Internet." J Pers Soc Psychol. 2000 Nov;79(5):748-62. PubMed PMID: 11079239. www.ncbi.nlm.nih.gov/pubmed/11079239?dopt=Abstract. Accessed July 2019.

51. von Mohr, Mariana et al. "The soothing function of touch: affective touch reduces feelings of social exclusion." Scientific reports vol. 7,1 13516. 18 Oct. 2017, doi:10.1038/s41598-017-13355, www.ncbi.nlm.nih.gov/pmc/articles/PMC5647341/ Accessed July 2019.

52. Reiner, Andrew. "The Power of Touch, Especially for Men." *New York Times*, December 5, 2017, www.nytimes.com/2017/12/05/well/family/gender-men-touch.html Accessed July 2019.

53. Killam, Kasley. "A Hug a Day Keeps the Doctor Away." *Scientific American*, March 17, 2015, www.scientificamerican.com/article/a-hug-a-day-keeps-the-doctor-away/ Accessed July 2019.

54. Pappas, Stephanie. "Oxytocin: Facts About the 'Cuddle Hormone'" *Live Science*, June 04, 2015, www.livescience.com/42198-what-is-oxytocin.html Accessed July 2019.

Chapter 4

55. *Me too.* https://metoomvmt.org/about/. Accessed May 2020

56. Watson, Andrew. "Handshakes at the Door: Hype, or Helpful?" *Learning and the Brain Blog*, June 3, 2019, www.learningandthebrain.com/blog/handshakes-at-the-door-hype-or-helpful/, Accessed July 2019

57. Grewen KM, Girdler SS, Amico J, Light KC. "Effects of partner support on resting oxytocin, cortisol, norepinephrine, and blood pressure before and after warm partner contact." *Psychosom Med.* 2005 Jul-Aug;67(4):531-8. PubMed PMID: 16046364. www.ncbi.nlm.nih.gov/pubmed/16046364

58. Sarda-Joshi, Gauri. "11 Science-Backed Truths on the Power of Human Touch." *Brain Fodder*,

brainfodder.org/11-studies-human-touch/ Accessed July 2019.

59. Chillot, Rick. "The Power of Touch" *Psychology Today*. March 2013, Rev. November 21, 2019. www.psychologytoday.com/gb/articles/201303/the-power-touch

60. Chillot, Rick. "The Power of Touch" *Psychology Today*. March 2013, Rev. November 21, 2019. www.psychologytoday.com/gb/articles/201303/the-power-touch

61. Ruiz, Don Miguel, Jr. *The Four Agreements: Practical Guide to Personal Freedom (Toltec Wisdom)*. Amber-Allen Publishing, Incorporated, 1997.

Chapter 5

62. Field, Tiffany. *Touch, second edition*, Kindle, The MIT Press, 2014.

63. Chillot, Rick. "The Power of Touch" *Psychology Today*. March 2013, Rev. November 21, 2019. www.psychologytoday.com/gb/articles/201303/the-power-touch, Accessed November 2019.

64. Floyd, Kory. "Relational and Health Correlates of Affection Deprivation." *Western Journal of Communication*, 2014, www.researchgate.net/publication/271931280_Relational_and_Health_Correlates_of_Affection_Deprivation, Accessed July 2019.

65. Henley, N.M. "Status and sex: Some touching observations." *Bull. Psychon. Soc.* 2, 91–93 (1973),

Published November 27, 2013, DOI 10.3758/BF03327726, https://link.springer.com/article/10.3758/BF03327726, Accessed July 2019

66. Reiner, Andrew. "The Power of Touch, Especially for Men." *The New York Times,* December 5, 2017, www.nytimes.com/2017/12/05/well/family/gender-men-touch.html, Accessed August 2019

67. Floyd, Kory. "Relational and Health Correlates of Affection Deprivation." *Western Journal of Communication,* 2014. 78:4, 383-403, DOI: 10.1080/10570314.2014.927071.

68. "Social isolation, loneliness in older people pose health risks." April 23, 2019, www.nia.nih.gov/news/social-isolation-loneliness-older-people-pose-health-risks. Cacioppo S, Capitanio JP, Cacioppo JT. "Toward a neurology of loneliness." *Psychol Bull.* 2014;140(6):1464-1504. doi:10.1037/a0037618. Accessed November 2019

69. Mesch, Gustavo & Talmud, Ilan. "Online Friendship Formation, Communication Channels, and Social Closeness." *International Journal of Internet Science.* 1, 2006. www.researchgate.net/publication/26495342_Online_Friendship_Formation_Communication_Channels_and_Social_Closeness, Accessed July 2019

70. Ausburn, Deborah, A. "'No-Touch' Policies Harm Children." *Taylor English Youth Services Law Blog.* January 9, 2019, www.taylorenglish.com/blogs-youth-services,no-touch-policies-harm-children, Accessed July 2019

71. Brown, Brené. "Getting Curious." *Rising Strong,* Kindle, Random House, LLC, 2015, pg 80.
72. Mills, Jen. "Most people want all physical contact banned at work, says survey." *Metro.* April 24, 2019, metro.co.uk/2019/04/24/people-want-physical-contact-banned-work-says-survey-9296001/, Accessed November 2019
73. Half, Robert. "Hugging Etiquette at Work: Advice from The Emily Post Institute." *Robert Half.com.* February 11,2019, www.roberthalf.com/blog/salaries-and-skills/hugging-etiquette-at-work-advice-from-the-emily-post-institute, Accessed November 2019
74. www.dictionary.com/browse/culture?s=t

Conclusion

75. Reger MA, Stanley IH, Joiner TE. "Suicide Mortality and Coronavirus Disease 2019—A Perfect Storm?" *JAMA Psychiatry*. Published online April 10, 2020. doi:10.1001/jamapsychiatry.2020.1060. Accessed May, 2020
76. Panchal, Nirmita, et al. "The Implications of COVID-19 for Mental Health and Substance Use." April 21, 2020, www.kff.org/coronavirus-covid-19/issue-brief/the-implications-of-covid-19-for-mental-health-and-substance-use/ Accessed May, 2020

77. "Aging Studies Expert: Social Distancing to Have Multiple Impacts on Older Adults." California State University, Fullerton, March 30, 2020, http://news.fullerton.edu/2020wi/Social-Distancing-Health-Impacts.aspx. Accessed May 2020

78. Campbell, Andrew M. "An increasing risk of family violence during the Covid-19 pandemic: Strengthening community collaborations to save lives." *Forensic Science International*: Reports vol. 2 (2020): 100089. doi:10.1016/j.fsir.2020.100089. Accessed May 2020

Made in the USA
Monee, IL
04 September 2020